Shift to the Future

Changing Images of Early Childhood
Series Editor: Nicola Yelland

Shift to the Future

Rethinking Learning with New Technologies in Education

Nicola Yelland

Routledge
Taylor & Francis Group
New York   London

Routledge is an imprint of the
Taylor & Francis Group, an informa business

Routledge
Taylor & Francis Group
270 Madison Avenue
New York, NY 10016

Routledge
Taylor & Francis Group
2 Park Square
Milton Park, Abingdon
Oxon OX14 4RN

© 2007 by Taylor & Francis Group, LLC
Routledge is an imprint of Taylor & Francis Group, an Informa business

Printed in the United States of America on acid-free paper
10 9 8 7 6 5 4 3 2 1

International Standard Book Number-10: 0-415-95319-7 (Softcover) 0-415-95318-9 (Hardcover)
International Standard Book Number-13: 978-0-415-95319-1 (Softcover) 978-0-415-95318-4 (Hardcover)

Library of Congress Cataloging-in-Publication Data

Yelland, Nicola.
    Shift to the future : rethinking learning with new technologies in education / Nicola Yelland.
        p. cm. -- (Changing images of early childhood)
    Includes bibliographical references and index.
    ISBN 0-415-95318-9 (hb) -- ISBN 0-415-95319-7 (pb)
    1. Early childhood education--Computer-assisted instruction. 2. Technology and children. 3. Educational technology. I. Title. II. Series.

LB1139.35.C64Y45 2006
372.134'4--dc22   2006009556

**Visit the Taylor & Francis Web site at
http://www.taylorandfrancis.com**

**and the Routledge Web site at
http://www.routledge-ny.com**

DEDICATION

For my children and their children . . .
education, education, education.

CONTENTS

FOREWORD

New technologies dazzle in one moment and prompt fear in another. They promise brighter futures but often seem to leave the world no better off, and sometimes worse off. Today we are in the midst of one of the most significant technological changes of all time, the information and communications technology revolution. This particular revolution is one that deeply implicates that most intimate and intrinsic of human of characteristics—our capacity to make meaning and to communicate. It is little wonder, then, that the sentiments that arise in our love-hate relationship with technology are at the forefront of our consciousness today, perhaps more intensely so than at any time in the past.

This book explores the actual and possible impacts of the new information and communications technologies on schools. As is the case in other realms of social activity, some are dazzled by the potential of the new technologies and by what the panoply of new devices and tools could contribute to students' learning. Some of the new technologies are specially designed for schools, such as learning management systems and learning objects. Others are general purpose tools, such as those for the digital capture, reproduction, and transmission of text, image, and sound. Still others, such as video games and the Internet, are so profoundly changing children's and adults' everyday lives that they are bound to influence education deeply.

The key question asked by this book is whether the new technologies are just new ways of doing old things or the beginning of something genuinely new. The old technologies of learning were pencils, exercise books, blackboards, and textbooks. Even the architecture of classrooms was a communications technology of sorts, with the teacher talking at the front and the students shooting up their hands, ready to answer the teacher's questions on cue. School has always been a place of technology, shaped as much by its spaces and artifacts as by anything else. In this book, Professor Yelland calls these the older technologies of learning "industrial age" schooling.

The new information and communications technologies are having such an impact on society that we might call our contemporary times an "information age" or "knowledge era." Professor Yelland's key thesis in this book is that "we should not be mapping the use of new technologies onto old curricula; rather, we need to rethink our curricula and pedagogies in light of the impact that we know new technologies can have on learning and meaning making in contemporary times."

Professor Yelland's focus is by no means that of a technological determinist or a technocrat. She speaks of the enormous potentials of the new technologies, but also of their dangers. Most importantly, she is more concerned with the human and learning relationships that enmesh and give meaning to the new technologies than with the technologies themselves. The new technologies can be used to replicate the worst of the old, lockstep, disciplinarian, content-transmission pedagogies of the industrial age. They are not in and of themselves an improvement to pedagogical relationships. Indeed, they can at times represent a distinct regression, depersonalizing and dehumanizing the learning process.

However, as this book so eloquently reveals, there is enormous potential in the new technologies to create innovative and more powerful learning more appropriate to a society that values creativity, innovation, and people who have an always-open attitude to learning new things. Not only do schools need to make themselves relevant to the new social world they inhabit, but they should seize the moment, taking this opportunity to reinvent themselves and reinvigorate learning.

This book weaves its way between big-picture analyses of the role of technology in our changing world and vividly concrete examples of how these changes are transforming the ways in which we teach and learn. On every page, it challenges our conventional thinking on learning and technology. The challenge is not only to understand the nature and depth of technological change. It is also a challenge to rethink the fundamentals of that most human of our capacities, our capacity to learn. This is a book every educator needs to read.

Mary Kalantzis
Professor and Dean, College of Education
University of Illinois at Urbana-Champaign

Bill Cope
Research Professor, Department of Educational Policy Studies
University of Illinois at Urbana-Champaign

ACKNOWLEDGMENTS

There are so many people who have influenced me and played a vital role in the work that is incorporated in this book. All the school-based examples provided in this book are from projects that were funded by the Australian Research Council (ARC), and I am deeply indebted to the scheme and its support from 1995 to the present day. I have had the pleasure of working on projects with so many talented people, namely (from the beginning): Jenny Masters, Doug Clements, Andee Rubin, Emma Cassidy, Liz Prenzler, Sue Grieshaber, Sue Hill, Libby Lee, Maureen O'Rourke, Yasmine Fauzee, Mary Kalantzis, and Bill Cope. Thanks to Anna Kilderry for her wonderful work in making detailed observations and notes in classrooms and from video data; it has made the research process so much richer. Kerry Wardlaw has worked with me for a year. Her writing and editing skills are invaluable, and her compilation of Chapter 7 is a vital contribution. Then there are those who gave me strength and encouraged me to persist, including my colleagues (in alphabetical order) Michael and Rima Apple, Anna Bower, Ray Brooks, Quentin Bryce, Dennis Cardinale, Iyla Davies, Shelley Dole, Glen Evans, Christy Falba, Alan Hayes, Peter Kell, Michele Knobel, Colin Lankshear, Mike Lawson, Vivienne (Wai Man) Leung, Bob Lingard, Allan Luke, Ronnie and George Lyons, Linda and Charlie Pulaski, Mike Singh, Gary Stager, Megan Thomas, Leanne Wiseman, and Karen Yuen; my family, Tamsyn and Caja, who have kept me strong and dedicated; and the women who inspired and shaped me, my grandmothers Gwendoline and Muriel, my mother Pat, and my aunt and godmother Stella. Thanks also to Catherine Bernard for her wit, valor, and incredible knowledge of publishing and editing. And last, but never least, I thank the wonderful children, teachers, and principals who have been so gracious in letting me into their lives and classrooms so that we could discover new things.

1

THE MILLENNIALS

The future is not what older people think but what younger people do.

—*Nicholas Negroponte*

INTRODUCTION

The children entering our schools today were born in the twenty-first century. These children are the youngest members of a group that ranges up to those who were born after 1985 and graduated from school in the past five years; they have come to be known as the "millennial generation" (Howe and Strauss 2000). These schoolchildren are experiencing a world that is vastly different from that of previous generations. Social, cultural, and technological conditions have transformed virtually every aspect of our lives, and it is hard to predict what life after school will be like for those five-year-olds who are just now entering our schools. Yet we claim that our education system is preparing them for life in a changing world, one in which they will have important roles to play as workers and citizens.

This book is concerned with children and learning and the optimal ways in which we can promote meaningful and useful learning in our schools in the twenty-first century. In doing this we should be concerned with creating contexts that enable children not only to acquire skills that will be relevant to their lives but also to retain their curiosity and creativity so that the foundations for lifelong and lifewide learning are established. My basic contention is that in the information age or knowledge era, we should not be mapping the use of new technologies onto old curricula; rather, we need to rethink our curricula and pedagogies in light of the impact that we know new technologies can have on learning and meaning making in contemporary times. The basic purpose of the book is to highlight some of the issues and provide examples from empirical research studies to illustrate the ways in which this can occur in classrooms and in out-of-school contexts that have an impact on what children do in schools. I use the terms "new technologies" and "learning technologies" interchangeably to include computers, digital cameras and televisions, MP3 players, mobile telephony, electronic whiteboards, scanners, electronic musical instruments (keyboards), and laser printers; I also extend these terms to the software that enables children to experience the process of education in new ways, such as the Internet, communications software such as Skype and Messenger, editing programs such as iMovie and Moviemaker, GarageBand, Kid Pix, and the suite of Microsoft programs that includes PowerPoint, Word, and Excel. All these things enable learners to function in new ways that were not possible prior to their introduction. They have also been collectively called information and communications technologies (ICT). Old technologies, by contrast, include pencils, crayons, pens, blackboards, textbooks, and overhead projectors.

Further, it will be suggested here that we need to reconsider what it means to become knowledgeable in the twenty-first century, and distinguish this from what held currency in previous eras. The current form of curricula across the world has remained relatively unchanged for centuries, yet increases in knowledge have been fundamental and significant. To accommodate new knowledge we have added to an already crowded curriculum while at the same time increasing the responsibility of schools to help children to understand issues around citizenship, sexuality, human relationships, being active and healthy, and preparing for the workplace. Consequently, we are not preparing the millennials for life in new times (Hall and Jacques 1989), and we are ignoring the lifeworlds that they inhabit, which are rich contexts for learning and saturated with new technologies.

Scardamalia (2003, 2) has suggested that we need to consider knowledge building as central to the education process in order to foster creativity and innovation, skills that are essential for effective functioning in the twenty-first century. She defines knowledge building as:

> the production and continual improvement of ideas of value to a community, through means that increase the likelihood that what the community accomplishes will be greater than the sum of individual contributions and part of broader cultural efforts . . . [A]s applied to education . . . the approach means engaging learners in the full process of knowledge creation.

Knowledge building should occur in all aspects of learners' lives and is not restricted to school. This is important, since the learning that children bring to school from their homes and communities needs to be valued and extended. In this model schools become places where public knowledge is explored, experimented with, and modified in dynamic ways, and thus the boundaries of what we know are extended. Children of the twenty-first century are able to embrace the notion as they are growing up with the capacity to experience and construct new meanings from the process.

THE MILLENNIALS AND NEW TECHNOLOGIES AND MEDIA

The millennials have grown up with an increasing array of technologies that they use fluently. The Kaiser Family Foundation (2005) has conducted two major studies with American students confirming that kids grow up literally surrounded by media and that even the very youngest (two years of age) are exposed to media on a daily basis. For example, American children spent 6.5 hours a day using media in 2005, and none of this occurred in school. Interestingly, the studies found that most kids also still read for fun, using new media to supplement rather than replace other, more traditional media. Thus "kids who spend a lot of time with one kind of media—whether it is TV, computers, or books—tend to spend a lot of time with all kinds of media" (Kaiser Family Foundation 1999, 31). Another interesting finding from the 2005 survey was that about a quarter of the sample reported using two types of media simultaneously, such as listening to music while working on the computer or reading a magazine while watching TV. Neither report found evidence to support the notion that this generation was addicted to computers or video games. However, both noted that while computers and TV were the most frequently used media, the children also engaged with a variety of other media in their out-of-school lives. Accordingly, the later study reported:

> Contrary to most expectations, it does not appear that spending time with media takes away from the time children spend in other pursuits; in fact, it seems that those young people who spend the most time using media are also those whose lives are the most full with family, friends, and other interests. (Kaiser Family Foundation 2005, 14)

The two reports indicated that although the range of media in children's lives continues to expand, the total amount of time children spend with media has remained essentially the same over the five-year period.

More media are now present in the child's bedroom, and the simultaneous use of two or more media was more prevalent in 2005 (26 percent) than in 1999 (16 percent). The most noticeable difference between the data from the two studies was the increase in use of computers to access the Internet. The proportion of students with computers at home rose from 73 percent in 1999 to 86 percent in 2005, and home Internet access increased from 47 percent in 1999 to 74 percent in 2005. Additionally, the amount of time spent using a computer for other than schoolwork more than doubled, from twenty-seven minutes to just over an hour.

The later report's conclusion bears testimony to the lives of young people in the twenty-first century: "The sheer amount of time young people spend with media makes it plain that the potential for media to influence significant aspects of their lives should not be ignored" (Kaiser Family Foundation 2005, 39).

GLOBAL EDUCATIONAL POLICIES AND IMPERATIVES

Governments around the world seem to recognize that it is politically viable to support the growth and use of new technologies in educational contexts while simultaneously supporting those who call for a back-to-basics approach to literacy and numeracy. For example, the U.S. Department of Education noted that

> American education is being bolstered by the increasing use of educational technology, greater accountability, and growing new partnerships between tech-savvy students and teachers. . . . [T]he technology that has so dramatically changed the world outside our schools is now changing the learning and teaching environment within them. (U.S Department of Education 2005)

This acknowledgment of the importance of new media in all aspects of children's lives and the ways in which it has fundamentally changed how work is conducted, as well as the impact on both leisure and communication, is reflected in the focus of the new technology plan for the United States. It is based on seven recommendations that are aimed at preparing American children to be leaders in the twenty-first century:

- An investment in leadership so that "tech-savvy" leaders who can initiate partnerships with communities and industry to promote creativity and empower student learning are in place in schools
- Innovative budgeting that will enable schools to keep their technology current

- Improvements in teacher education so that new teachers can effectively use new technologies for educative purposes and are able to continue their professional education online
- Support for e-learning and virtual schools so that every American child has access to quality education that can be accredited to national standards
- Ensuring that schools have effective broadband access for teaching, learning, and assessment purposes with appropriate technical support
- Utilization of innovative digital content that complements national standards
- Integration of data systems so that planning and other administrative functions are streamlined and can support assessment and the communication of results

The U.S. Department of Education seems to be foregrounding a major change in focus that utilizes new technology extensively and suits contemporary times. Yet the recommendation must be understood within the context of the No Child Left Behind Act (U.S. Department of Education 2001), which ensures that the focus of schooling is related to an increase in accountability for student performance that is based *solely* on state reading and mathematics assessments, that is, tests. The policy document stipulates that there should be an increase in funds for technology. However, this goal is related not to encouraging the innovative use of creative ideas via the use of new technologies but rather to minimizing the paperwork associated with applying for funding for machines. The sections entitled "Improving Literacy by Putting Reading First" and "Improving Math and Science Instruction" reveal that the primary strategy for the former is connected to the introduction of a new program called Reading First, which is promoted as "a science-based program" (p. 10), while the latter goal involves plans to use experts from the university system to ensure that the "right" knowledge is being transmitted to students by people who know it, that is, *not* teachers in American schools. Children can easily be tested to determine whether they have acquired the knowledge specified in both; they demonstrate that they have done so by recalling the facts on the day of the test. It thus involves the measurement of specific literacy skills (e.g., reading, comprehension, and spelling) and mathematics and science knowledge that is considered to be as essential today as it was in previous times. There is recognition that "schools should use technology as a tool to improve academic achievement, and that using the latest technology in the classroom should not be an end unto itself" (p. 22). In this way it might be surmised that software that drills the basic skills of reading and mathematics is to be encouraged, since "states will be encouraged to set performance goals to measure how federal technology funds are being used to improve student achievement" (p. 23). This has to be viewed in the context of a document in which student achievement is considered only in terms of demonstrated proficiency in reading (a narrow definition of literacy) and mathematics. Accordingly, the No Child Left Behind document seems to epitomize the notion of "back to basics" because it pares schooling right down to these performance elements and in doing so claims to protect children and their parents from the vagaries of educational fads, which are considered to be the major contribution to the "disappointing results" of America's schoolchildren in international tests of literacy and numeracy.

In the United Kingdom the party currently in power, the Labour Party, was elected on a platform of "education, education, education" that was based on the notion that our "children cannot be effective in tomorrow's world if they are trained in yesterday's skills" (DFEE 1997, 1). Additionally, the European Union (EU) has increasingly supported the notion that the impact of technology on all our lives is significant: "This revolution adds huge new capacities to human intelligence and constitutes a resource which changes the way we work together and the way we live together" (Bangemann 1994).

However, the rhetoric does not seem to match reality, since throughout the world adults from all walks of life frequently describe the young people of today in terms of what they cannot do, such as focus on one thing at a time, spell basic words, remember historical facts, and add up numbers without using a calculator. Yet there is no evidence to support the notion that academic standards have fallen. To the contrary, Howe and Strauss reported that "during the 1990s, aptitude test scores have risen within every racial and ethnic groups, especially in elementary schools" (2000, 9). This is reinforced by David Berliner, who contended:

> Today's students average about 14 IQ points higher than their grandparents did and about 7 points higher than their parents did. . . . The number of students with IQs above 145 is now about 18 times greater than it was two generations ago. (Cited in Howe and Strauss 2000, 22)

There is no doubt that the children in our schools today are tested more than any previous generation, and there has been a sharp increase in support for more homework, longer school days, and traditional curricula. The No Child Left Behind policy (U.S. Department of Education 2001) has created an industry around test and practice materials that has now reached $200 million in annual sales (Howe and Strauss 2000, 159) and the form and content of these tests are structured so that they can be marked by machines: most questions are multiple-choice, and pieces of short writing are graded according to rigid guidelines that allow no leeway for creativity. In the Western world the importance of tests has galvanized parents and politicians to call for a return to traditional teaching in which phonics and the mechanics of mathematics (addition, subtraction) are foregrounded and there is no time for engagement with ideas and knowledge building; rather, the teaching of facts and information is increasingly filling up an already crowded curriculum.

This situation is critiqued by Schank:

> School isn't really about learning; it's about short-term memorization of meaningless information that never comes up later in life. The school model was never intended to help people acquire practical skills. It is intended to satisfy observers that knowledge is being acquired (for short periods of time). (2002, 7)

EDUCATION FOR THE TWENTY-FIRST CENTURY

It is often claimed that the purpose of education is to prepare people for life. Western education systems would seem to have been quite successful in preparing students to become workers to occupy the different strata of old or industrial capitalism. At the production level were jobs that required the use of basic skills in a routine manner without questioning the protocols or instructions. The managerial class had more schooling, so they were able to experience and recall more information that might be used to set them apart from those they managed. However, economic, social, and cultural conditions have changed, and the new global capitalism, inspired by scientific and technological advances, has made unnecessary many of the old industrial jobs or has outsourced them to developing countries, where labor costs a tenth of what it does in the West. The new era gives premiums to those citizens who are able to be creative, innovative, and transformative in their use of knowledge and skills in order to create new products, ideas, and services. This group is able to work abstractly and efficiently and adapt to changing times with fluency. At the opposite end of the spectrum are the workers who are increasingly being characterized as contract, temporary, manual, and itinerant or migrant; they rarely share in the benefits of the new capitalism but in fact are the major contributors to its success.

Schools are still set up for the old capitalism, while society and the economies of the world need them to produce workers for the new capitalism. Therein lies the paradox, because the same governments that want their countries to be leaders in design technologies, with the associated successes of creative, innovative products that feed the consumer market and lead to advances in science and medicine, simultaneously promote schooling that requires rote learning of skills and information, which they require to be demonstrated by competence in tests that can be internationally benchmarked and which serve as a measure of success for the system.

Those interested in preparing our children to live meaningful lives in the twenty-first century have argued that education should be about providing contexts in which students are able to acquire and practice (new) skills in ways that help them utilize existing ideas to generate new knowledge. This can be achieved by participating in inquiries that are authentic and engaging, collaborating with others, seeking out expert assistance and knowledge from a variety of sources, and communicating or disseminating the findings to others in an effective and appropriate way. Paradoxically, employers in the twenty-first century have also indicated that this is what they need in the workforce, while simultaneously reinforcing the opinion that the young people of today are not able to spell, add, or complete simple forms. It is apparent that being able to generate, think, inquire, collaborate, critique, and communicate ideas and knowledge is relevant to all disciplines or domains of knowledge. These can be regarded as the new basics of the twenty-first century. Our education system remains structured around bodies of facts that need to be known and regurgitated periodically and thus is failing the next generation in serious and fundamental ways. It occurs despite the fact that we have a great deal of information from numerous research projects about the ways in which new technologies are able to transform learning (e.g., Yelland 1997; Tinker 1999).

Theories of learning (e.g., Bruner 1977; Piaget 1972; Vygotsky 1978) that underpin Western education systems are grounded in the belief that humans learn best when they are engaged and actively constructing meaning. They need to be able to do this in an environment that supports their explorations and where they are able to learn from their mistakes. This means that children should be encouraged to take risks. We also need to realize that creativity and the generation of new knowledge and procedures for exploring will arise only when learners are encouraged in a supportive environment, one in which they are able to feel free to express their opinions and justify their responses in appropriate ways.

More than twenty-five years ago Papert (1980) outlined a vision for educators that encouraged the use of technology to support intellectual engagement with ideas and thinking. Papert's notion of using machines as objects to think with was powerful since he contended that knowledge that was abstract and previously inaccessible to young children could be experienced "concretely," thus opening up new horizons for learners. Cuban (1993) has noted that this has not in fact happened and education has remained much the same, in terms of the content of curriculum and the types or methods of teaching that are used, despite advances in the use of new technologies. Thus while there is a recognition that these are "new times" (Hall and Jacques 1989), characterized by dynamic changes in all facets of our lives that have moved us away from the "old times" dominated by the Fordist factory model, which required the use of workers in a mechanistic and rote manner, the reality is that schools and the curricula that exist today are more suited to the needs of the industrial age than those of the information age.

The dynamics of globalization require rethinking of our everyday lifeworlds and the impact that we may have on others. This of course includes recognition of diversity across contexts, cultures, identities, commerce, and production. The role of new technologies in our lives has significantly reshaped our lifeworlds: jobs have been obliterated, and new ways of living require different things from us. Many millennials have already been inducted into new systems as citizens, workers, and consumers. As societies have evolved to accommodate these massive changes, the world's education systems seem to have maintained their traditional and national characteristics. This can be clearly seen in neoliberal and neo-conservative attitudes (e.g., Apple 2001) and in pedagogies influenced by those who think that education systems should be structured and assessed via tests, through measurable outcomes, and by strict adherence to standards that are overt and efficient (e.g., U.S. Department of Education 2001).

For many students and educators, the resultant curricula and educational experiences have been narrowed and reduced to prescribed outcomes limited to testing a small range of behaviors that are supposed to indicate the possession of content and skills more suited to the industrial age rather than the information age, as previously stated. In this educational climate, modernist notions of universality and reason have prevailed and the potential for discovery and progression into areas epitomized by new learning initiatives is valued only if scientifically tested. Thus grand narratives (Lyotard 1984) continue to dominate the educational agenda, and as a consequence, arguments about "back to basics," "grading kindergarten," and "no child left behind" are promulgated to defend testing and stringent accountability measures. These mantras and their associated practices, whether in the form of adherence to rigid curriculum discipline areas within the school sector or in the formation of "child-centered" curricula in the early years, reflect systems that have resisted change. They represent the ways in which the traditional nature and structure of education has been sanctified and maintained.

Yet there are those who question the credibility and viability of these approaches as the foundation for education systems. Increasingly, educators recognize that lifeworlds have become complex and require new forms of analysis, description, and practice. Postmodern perspectives are characterized by heterogeneity, multiple discourses, awareness of the complexity of diversity, and emancipation through critiques of universal truths and structures (e.g., Harvey 1989). In their rejection of reason, based on empirical evidence, postmodern scholars offer views that are often complex and challenging and not always definitive. This is frequently problematic for those people in education who pride themselves on being pragmatists and want to know what is best for the children in their care. Postmodern analyses and critiques do not often offer solutions or prescriptions for success. However, in providing the means of interrogating educational contexts in which we find ourselves, such perspectives (e.g., poststructuralist, feminist, and postcolonial) and techniques (e.g., deconstruction and discourse analysis) have encouraged alternative viewpoints, which in turn have resulted in renewed practices in some schools.

It is increasingly evident that unless schools address the notion of diversity and the ways in which learners engage with ideas and experiences, they will not remain relevant to the lives of students. The challenge is, of course, how to make education relevant for a diverse population so that it is possible for each person to engage and, as a consequence, learn. As Kalantzis and Cope commented:

> Learning succeeds or fails to the extent that it engages the varied subjectivities of learners. Engagement produces opportunity, equity and participation. Failure to engage produces failure, disadvantage and inequality.... [E]ngagement must be with learners in their lifeworld reality, and that reality is marked by extraordinary difference. (2005, 46–47)

ACCESS AND EQUITY

The notion of a "digital divide" has highlighted the major differences between the haves and have-nots in terms of access to and use of new technologies and the ways in which some groups of citizens are limited in their potential to engage and participate in new ways of thinking and being in the twenty-first century.

A recognition of diversity and issues around globalization, social justice, and equity are fundamental to the issues associated with the ownership and use of new technologies. Discussion around the issues is important and complex, since it is not only about providing machines for a particular group who may be considered to be disenfranchised in the information revolution. It has been suggested that the debate "is woven in a complex manner into social systems and processes" (Warschauer 2004, 8). In various examples of attempts to breach or eliminate the digital divide the emphasis has been on the need to provide machines for people. This has led to a focus on the technology rather than on the actions that are possible as a result of it and the ways in which these are able to transform lives. Warschauer argues for the use of the term social inclusion, which not only aligns with contemporary policy imperatives around the globe but also enables us to engage with important issues around identity, language, social participation, community, and effective citizenship. One important aspect of the digital divide is that it has facilitated or instigated discussions around making access to new technologies an issue since it has been apparent that such divisions occur within nation-states as well as across continents. For example, the Kaiser Family Foundation (2005), in its survey of media use by young people in the United States, reported that the majority of youth from each of the ethnic and socioeconomic groups studied had Internet access at home and that the increase from the Foundation's 1999 survey was higher among people of color and those from lower socioeconomic levels. Still, the study maintained that the gulf between people of different races and social groups remains significant. It cites the 80 percent rate of access to the Internet by Caucasian students in the home, compared to 61 percent for African Americans. Further, when the researchers asked about going online in a typical day, 54 percent of students living in communities where median income was less than $35,000 a year reported they could do this, compared to 71 percent where the median income was greater than $50,000.

However, a focus on the machines without considering the social context and applications that are possible with them is based on a limited understanding of how individuals might make sense of their world and acquire the social capital relevant to participating effectively as citizens in society. In much of the literature technologies are regarded merely as *tools*. Yet, as Castells (1996) has noted, technologies are also *processes* that affect how we can make sense of the world and communicate our views to others about it, and this impacts on knowledge building in new and dynamic ways. This view places the learner as active and constructive in doing things that have an effect on outcomes (i.e., knowledge creation), rather than just as a user or consumer of technology. It is important since it implies different levels of agency and seems to align with Papert's (1980) goal for the use of computers, in that he wanted students to be in control of the machine and not vice versa.

Warschauer (2004, 38) has suggested that access to ICT and literacy are similar in a number of ways. For example, "literacy and ICT access are closely connected to advances in human communication and the means of knowledge production." ICT and literacy access are both prerequisites for "full participation in the informational age of capitalism," just as literacy was essential to the earlier industrial stages. Also, both literacy and ICT access require the use of a physical object (e.g., a book or computer) so that connections can be made its content, and also require particular skills necessary to derive new understandings from it. Literacy and ICT require learners to both receive and produce information. Finally, literacy and ICT are connected to issues around diversity and inequality since fluency in either or both can influence individual expectations and achievements (Warschauer 2004, 38–39).

Lankshear and Knobel have noted that while "numerous highly influential (and powerful) literacies exist that enjoy high-profile places within contemporary everyday culture . . . [they] are not in any significant way accounted for in school learning" (2003, 24). This chasm between children's lives and school experiences is discussed in more detail in Chapter 4. However, it is evident that many of the things we do in real life are frequently ignored in school life: for example, students are still required to handwrite texts before typing them, and they also spend inordinate amounts of time manually operating on numbers that they would use a calculator for in other situations. In this way, the relevance of school will be continually be brought into question by students whose daily lives are growing increasingly different from what they are experiencing in their classrooms. Their school contexts often ignore the use of new technologies and the associated processes that are inherent to them, or use them to support traditional practices in irrelevant ways. Even for schools that have a high saturation of computers this remains a problem. If, as the statistics seem to reveal, richer countries or more affluent suburbs have more machines, it does not necessarily follow that they are being used in ways that are appropriate to the needs and interests of their students. In fact, it might be the case that schools with the most traditional curricula do not support learning with new technologies. The work of Cuban (2001) has highlighted that without due consideration of the work of teachers and a broader vision of the role of schools in a democratic society the use of new technologies will have a minimal impact on teaching and learning despite their ubiquitous use in our lives outside of schooling.

If education is about preparing citizens of the future to lead productive and useful lives as well as to experience a sense of well-being, it is not just the presence of new technologies in school that will support this goal. It requires a fundamental shift in how we conceptualize curricula and the pedagogies that are deployed to maximize learning. It is futile to ask what the impact of computers is on learning outcomes. This technologically deterministic perspective has been equated with the "fire" model of educational technology, that is, the idea that "a computer in the classroom will automatically generate learning in the same way that a fire automatically generates heat" (Warschauer 2004, 202).

Warschauer (2004) goes on to point out that technologies are not neutral, since their presence and use bring certain values and assumptions to learning contexts that cannot be, or should not be, ignored. For example, experiences with computers are fundamentally shaped and determined by the dominant discourses associated with communicating in English. Warschauer relates the story of the development of the initial coding system for computers (American Standard Code for Information Exchange, ASCII), which allowed for only the representation of the English alphabet in upper- and lowercase with standard punctuation marks. There was no way to accommodate the diacritical marks of many of the European languages, and the symbol systems of the non-Roman-alphabet languages were totally ignored. Thus, English as the medium of communication was privileged from the beginning and now is so firmly entrenched that it continues to dominate not only access to and use of the Internet but also the publication of materials (e.g., books, videos, and DVDs), which consequently impacts on the status of the broader social systems and structures of English-speaking countries and their citizens. As Warschauer noted, "The significance of coding and other design issues once again demonstrates the complex interrelationship of technology and society in contrast to a simplistic notion of outside impacts" (2004, 204).

This complex interrelationship extends to our understandings about the role of technology not only in education but also in our lives. Technology has changed virtually everything we do: facilitating communication so that we can send e-mails and get instantaneous replies from anywhere in the world, changing our shopping practices, and saving hours of time on mundane and routine tasks such as washing clothes and dishes. Our lives will never be the same again in terms of this impact— few want to return to the good old days of washing sheets and towels by hand, for example. However, what has happened in education is that the new technologies are peripheral to the main activity, which is still heavily reliant on old technologies and traditional ways of knowing. They have had little impact on styles of teaching or reshaped what we do and value in schools. This is bizarre in many ways, since as Postman noted, "A new technology does not add or subtract something. It changes everything. In the year 1500, fifty years after the printing press was invented, we did not have old Europe plus the printing press. We had a *different* Europe" (Postman 1993, 18; italics added).

A useful way of considering the uses of new technologies for learning is provided by Warschauer (2004) as a sociotechnical model for ICT that can be contrasted to the traditional way in which ICT is regarded. The application of the model has important ramifications for the ways in which we attempt to incorporate ICT in models of schooling. In the model the following features are evident:

- ICT is regarded as a sociotechnical network (not just a tool) that will be implemented with particular plans in mind (e.g., a business plan) but also needs an ecological perspective (i.e., a human and environmental dimension).
- ICT implementation involves more than the presence of new machines, since their effects are often indirect and related to social, economic, and political considerations.
- Incentives to change practices often require rethinking aspects of work and workplace cultures.
- Relationship building is an important and inherent part of the success (or lack of success) of implementation.
- There is recognition of the social, economic, and political ramifications of the use of the technology for all aspects of work and life.
- Contexts in which the technology will be used are complex ("e.g., matrices of business, services, people, technology, history, location").
- Knowledge and expertise are regarded as being connected.
- Infrastructures should be in place and need to be supported with additional processes for successful implementation.

This perspective on the use of new technologies reinforces the view that it is not the machines but what individuals or groups do with them that is relevant to social change and important for social inclusion. It moves us away from a "tool" view of technology to what Kling and Scacchi (1982) refer to as a "package" model, in which technology is more than a physical device . . . [it] includes not only the hardware and software, but also a diverse set of skills, organizational units to supply and maintain computer-based services and data, and sets of beliefs about what computing is good for and how it may be used efficaciously. (1982, 6)

In this way the original notion of the digital divide, which was useful in highlighting the inequity of computer access, now needs to be reconsidered in light of the huge social, economic, and political importance that the use of the machines implies. As Warschauer points out, "The overall policy challenge is not to overcome a digital divide but rather to expand access to and use of ICT for promoting social inclusion" (2004, 211).

From this viewpoint, access to and use of ICT involve conceptualizing machines in a different way so that we take account of the processes inherent in their use. When ICT is used to glitz up mundane school tasks, it does not empower learners or afford the opportunity for them to do things in innovative ways. For example, the Internet is not just a place where you can find out stuff; it is a space that enables and extends experiences. It has the ability to transform what we know by making information easier to find and changing how we are able to operate with it. Those who are excluded from this process for whatever reason are being denied the social capital that comes with being able to synthesize and transform this into knowledge that is socially, economically, or politically useful.

The data from the United States were similar to those reported in a major study that was conducted in the United Kingdom (Becta 2002) that found home ownership of computers and access to the Internet were increasing. Yet 25 percent of the 2,100 pupils surveyed still did not have access to the Internet at home. Despite there being access for them in places such as libraries and Internet cafes, these were expensive options, and their locations and times of opening often were not ideal. In this way students without access to the Internet at home were considered to be disadvantaged, since they were disenfranchised from the activities inherent to Internet use that enabled them "to develop skills and literacies in networked ICT, [become] confident in its use, and [develop] a range of on-line social and communication skills" (Becta 2002, 2).

The study also provided data to illustrate that respondents were "aware of the moral and ethical debates surrounding the use of networked technologies and the perceived security risks" (Becta 2002, 3). This was in a context in which they spent a lot more time on computers at home than in schools; at home they felt they had "greater autonomy" (p. 2) to explore ICT effectively and for sustained periods of time without interruption. This meant that they came to school with a higher level of skills and deeper understandings about issues than their teachers anticipated, and this of course had important repercussions for their feelings about their experiences with ICT in classrooms.

The report suggested that "schools need to develop strategies for 'bridging the gap' for those pupils who do not have access to ICT resources, including the Internet, at home" (Becta 2002, 3). It noted that it might be useful to educate parents about the benefits of ownership and connection to the Internet at home via subsidized leasing arrangements, since a major finding of the study was that "home use of the networked technologies such as web sites supports both self-directed and school-directed learning" (p. 16).

Discussion around the issues of Internet use in schools is complex. Many authorities and schools have screening or blocking software that controls access and in doing so restricts the powerful potential of the Internet as a source of information. Blanket restrictions often apply to sites that have keywords considered to be unsafe by some adults, who take the view that children need to be protected from the "dangerous" elements in society. On the surface this might seem to be reasonable, but in fact, as Katz suggests, "blocking software gives the illusion of control. It doesn't ensure safety since sophisticated evildoers will circumvent it even more quickly than kids. And it doesn't teach citizenship in the digital world" (Katz 1997).

Recently I was in a school where ten-year-old students were required to provide detailed information about the circulatory and respiratory systems, structured around some basic questions. They were able to use search engines to find the content they needed, and many were familiar with using Google, so they were quite adept at phrasing their requests. I suggested that with Google images it might be possible for the learners to find diagrams that would aid their narrative reports; since both systems are complex, pictures would be useful in understanding them. We then discovered that schools in the state had been advised to block this feature of the search engine, and as a consequence the students were limited in their capacity to use all the information available on the Internet. In talking with the principal later I asked whether it might be more appropriate to talk with the students and their families at the start of the year regarding appropriate and inappropriate uses of the Internet and enter into a social contract to be signed by all to endorse the decision made. He told me that he was not able to do this since the restriction on using Google images was a mandate from the state's Department of Education. At the same time he recognized that the decision restricted the students' potential learning. What is this teaching our children? Wouldn't it be better, as Katz advocates, to trust our children more, since "blocking deprives children of the opportunity to confront the realities of new culture: some of it is pornographic, violent, occasionally even dangerous. They need to master those situations in a rational, supervised way to learn how to truly protect themselves" (Katz 1997). We will return to discuss some potential alternatives to this decision in Chapter 6.

CREATING CONTEXTS FOR KNOWLEDGE-BUILDING COMMUNITIES IN THE INFORMATION AGE

Living in the twenty-first century means that we need to be able to deal with vast amounts of data and information and have the ability to absorb, synthesize, and transfer it into knowledge and understandings that have relevance to our lives. We live in a "data-drenched" society (Steen 1999) full of "data smog" (Shenk 1997), which suggests that it is hard to negotiate meaning in the face of such massive quantities of information. Making sense of data and information and using it to generate and solve problems and to process existing knowledge as well as to create contexts for generating new knowledge should be a fundamental goal of education today. Yet we remain focused on the recall of information as facts since these are easily tested and help politicians to report the perceived successes of their policies in simple terms with statistics that never tell the whole story. A report in the *South China Morning Post* (Forestier and Chan 2004), for example, reveals that once again students from Hong Kong outperformed nearly all of their Western counterparts in mathematics and science, according to the Trends in Mathematics and Science Study (TIMSS). However, while test scores were high, Hong Kong students' self confidence and enjoyment in learning were among the lowest in the world. A similar finding was evident for another international test, the Programme for International Student Assessment (PISA), where despite coming in first in the world in mathematics, Hong Kong students "had the worst perception of their schooling" (Forestier and Chan 2004). It would seem relevant to ask about the priorities of the system that produces such anomalies. Negroponte has suggested:

> The heavy price paid in countries like France, South Korea, and Japan for shoving many facts into young minds is often to have students more or less dead on arrival when they enter the university system. Over the next four years they feel like marathon runners being asked to go rock climbing at the finish line.

In rethinking our practices in curriculum and pedagogy, we need to consider the ways in which individuals can build knowledge via active exploration in areas that children have defined themselves, as well as responding to the needs of others in problem-solving and problem-posing contexts. It is relevant to think of children as learners who are engaged in using existing knowledge, extending or innovating current knowledge, and creating new knowledge for specific purposes that they have defined. It is also essential that learners be provided with opportunities to share their strategies and to communicate and disseminate their ideas. This is important for the creation of knowledge-building communities, and because we can learn a great deal from each other about the varied processes and strategies used, in order to evaluate their effectiveness. Scardamalia has commented that living in the knowledge society requires several things:

- Moving beyond brainstorming to bringing ideas into the world
- Producing knowledge that brings value to a community, which means going beyond merely "keeping abreast of the times"
- Developing understandings about knowledge creation
- Allowing individuals to take charge of knowledge at the highest level by playing with ideas

This book will provide some examples and describe scenarios to show how this might look in schools and will discuss the ways in which it would impact on our conceptualizations of curriculum and pedagogy.

Chapter 2 begins the process by exploring some of the contemporary contexts for learning. It considers ways in which a number of education departments have reconceptualized curricula so that they are able to prepare people to participate effectively as citizens in the twenty-first century. These curricula have been carefully planned and aligned with the evaluation and assessment of students in diverse ways. The chapter reviews and examines these in terms of their potential to promote new learning that meets the needs of the millennial workforce as well as providing environments that encourage learning, engagement with ideas, and generation of new knowledge. Additionally, professional organizations have supported innovations in teaching and learning in their relevant domains, as demonstrated by the case of the National Council for Teachers of Mathematics (NCTM), which provides examples from classroom learning in mathematics to illustrate the ways in which young learners can engage with concepts in new ways that incorporate the use of ICT.

Chapter 3 describes common early play experiences and reveals that children are immersed in big ideas and useful learning skills while playing. It considers the ways in which we might learn from this to make schools more meaningful learning places. It discusses the role of toys in preschool children's lives and the ways in which these have changed over time, presenting new opportunities for learning. This is placed in the context of active learning (constructivism) in vibrant social environments. Examples illustrate the ways in which young children learn in a variety of settings with a range of media. The multimodal nature of these experiences is highlighted, and the impact on creating contexts for new literacies and numeracies is explored.

Chapter 4 examines examples from a range of empirical research studies to illustrate the ways in which school-age children create and share knowledge in communities outside of school contexts. Data from studies about the informal learning of these children illustrate the powerful ways in which children engage with new technologies in and out of school and in community settings. This is linked to the examples provided in Chapter 5, which discusses new learning in schools with reference to specific empirical research studies.

Chapter 5 considers examples from school-based research projects in which children have worked on authentic learning tasks and activities in the context of the new curricula discussed in Chapter 2. These rich tasks show the ways in which a variety of new technologies, such as computers, cameras, software, the Internet, and games, have been used and serve to highlight the sophisticated knowledge that children are capable of creating and sustaining. These examples provide teachers and parents with research-based ideas for activities that are grounded in active construction of knowledge.

Chapter 6 synthesizes the main arguments and discusses the implications for the future of children. The stories and examples provided in the book underscore the optimistic conclusion that millennials will be able to reach their potential and will not need to say: "If the media focused on our achievements instead of our mistakes, then we would have something to aspire to" (Marjie Rosenfelt, cited in Howe and Strauss 2000, 18).

The final chapter, which was prepared and written by Kerry Wardlaw, provides sources of information for teachers, university educators, and parents about where they can locate more information as well as details of useful ideas for teaching and learning contexts. These resources build on the ideas presented in this book and correspond to each chapter heading, enabling the reader to expand on the research-based notions introduced in previous chapters.

This book is not advocating a technocratic view of education, in which new technologies assume the central role in the delivery of and participation in the educational experience. Rather, it asks readers to question how we shape and influence the education of the young people in our schools today. It has become increasingly evident that many young people think that schools are places they do not want to be, and one of the main reasons seems to be that they see no connection between schooling and their lives outside of it. However, in some instances this disconnection has emerged as aggression: Robinson (2001) highlights the disturbing statistic that in the United Kingdom 60 percent of teachers have reported that they would like to leave the profession, and one of the main reasons cited is the low level of discipline in the schools that they work in. If we believe that education is at the core of a successful society, then we should make schooling relevant to the lifeworlds of the children that attend them. This system cannot be based on an industrial model but needs to be reenvisioned for living in the digital world of the new knowledge society. This requires us to think differently about what it means to be an educated person and how citizens might make a contribution in the twenty-first century.

It is becoming increasingly evident that well-educated, creative, and innovative people who can work collaboratively and adapt to changing contexts are valued in the business world and are able to make substantial contributions in many spheres of life. This book presents and discusses some of the ways that have been tried in schools and in out-of-school contexts to illustrate the ways in which children can engage with powerful ideas and extend their knowledge base. In doing so it represents an opportunity to reflect both on what is and on what might be if schools focus on fostering the creative capacity of all children so that they feel valued and can participate in building skills and knowledge to ensure that they can be productive and interesting members of society.

2

NEW CONTEXTS FOR LEARNING

We are the seed of the new breed, we will succeed, our time has come.

—*East 17*

This chapter explores some of the ways in which education systems, professional organizations, and teachers have attempted to make what happens in classrooms around the world more relevant to the children who are in those classrooms every day. It begins by discussing the concept of New Times (Hall and Jacques 1989) and the ways in which education has the potential to address significant issues and create contexts for knowledge building. It then introduces the notion of new learning (ACDE 2001) and suggests ways this might be implemented in classrooms by exploring three different examples of initiatives. The first occurs at the state level with a reconceptualized curriculum. The next example was instigated by a professional organization, the National Council of the Teachers of Mathematics (NCTM), with the goal of making mathematics curricula more relevant and accountable in contemporary times. Changes in practice can also be initiated by teacher researchers, who, as reflective practitioners, realize that there is potential to make the lived experiences in their classrooms more relevant and thus provide fertile grounds for learning and engagement. Classroom-based studies provide empirical data to illustrate the ways in which teachers were able to innovate on their practice while participating in university-based research projects. Finally, ways of assessing learning within the context of these examples are provided so that teachers are able to realize the potential of learners and build on them in effective ways.

PREPARING CITIZENS FOR TOMORROW

In characterizing New Times, Hall and Jacques argued that the world has changed significantly in qualitative terms, with the standardization, homogeneity, and organizations of scale of modernity having been replaced by diversity, differentiation, and fragmentation. They view this as being exemplified by the shift from Fordism to post-Fordism, which is illustrated by a "much wider and deeper social and cultural development" (1989, 12). Hall and Jacques noted that the changes that created the context for New Times also resulted in the production of new social divisions; inequality and disempowerment still exist but are manifested in different ways. Basically, they contended, "New Times . . . is about making a new world" (p. 20), and one of the fundamental changes is related to work "being re-organised around new technology" (p. 33). This means that workers, at various levels in the workforce, now need to demonstrate that they can work in collaborative groups in a flexible and cohesive way with a high level of skill and knowledge specialization. Hall and Jacques contended that the presence and use of new technologies mean not simply that new skills and practices have been created but also that they require new ways of thinking:

> Modern technology, far from having a fixed path, is open to constant renegotiation and re-articulation. "Planning," in this new technological environment, has less to do with absolute predictability and everything to do with instituting a "regime" out of which a plurality of outcomes will emerge. One, so to speak, plans for contingency. This mode of thinking signals the end of a certain kind of deterministic rationality. (Hall and Jacques 1989, 129)

It is in this context that contemporary education systems both at the national and local levels, are slowly beginning to realize that we need to create new contexts for learning that are relevant and meaningful and which prepare students for New Times.

Scardamalia and Bereiter have suggested that "the health and wealth of societies depends increasingly on their capacity to innovate. People in general, not just a specialized elite, need to work creatively with knowledge" (2003, 1370). This has important ramifications for schooling, since the education system should enable students not only to be current in their knowledge but also to be able to generate new knowledge as part of their everyday experiences. It was recognized by Lyndon B. Johnson as far back as 1964 when he told an audience at the University of Michigan that "the Great Society is a place where every child can find knowledge to enrich his mind and to enlarge his talents" (Johnson 1964). To be relevant to future citizens, education should cater to their diverse life-worlds and recognize that the world has become increasingly complex. The old basics of reading, writing, and arithmetic that were taught by rote and practiced until mastery are not enough. These days an educated population needs to show the capacity to be innovative and creative, as well as being able to work collaboratively and flexibly on authentic tasks that have been generated by the students themselves as well as by teachers.

New technologies are an integral part of this learning. Technologies permeate the lives of the young people who attend our schools, yet within school they tend to remain peripheral to the main work that is done; in many cases their use is tokenistic rather than essential. In many schools educational computer games that can be described as "drill and practice" are frequently used to reinforce specific skills such as phonics in language lessons (e.g., Reader Rabbit Learn to Read with Phonics, Jump-Start Phonics) or mathematical operations such as practicing addition (e.g., Reader Rabbit Math, JumpStart Numbers, Math Workshop). This is not always a good strategy: mundane or routine activities are being introduced on the computer as a way of making them more interesting for children, but computer-based activities really aren't needed to practice such skills.

Thus while new technologies have revolutionized society, in schools their use has basically been to support traditional curricula and pedagogies rather than create new contexts for learning. This was clearly articulated by Papert when he criticized policy makers who were:

> determined to use computers but can only imagine using them in the framework of a school system as they know it; children following a predetermined curriculum mapped out year by year and lesson by lesson. This is quite perverse; new technology being used to strengthen a poor method of education that was invented only because there were no computers when school was designed. (1996, 25)

Cuban (1993) contended that there are two main reasons why schools have resisted the use of technology. The first lies in our conceptualization and cultural beliefs about the nature of teaching and learning, what knowledge is appropriate for studying in school, and the nature of the teacher-student relationship, which is central to the experience. Second, he maintained that the age-graded structure of schooling has been the major determinant that shaped the system and the deciding factor about what was taught and its timing in a carefully planned sequence of activity. Any innovation has to fit into this structure; otherwise it would be rejected.

Cuban asserted that there were three imperatives that coalesced in the desire to reform schools via ICT:

- Citizens should be prepared for life and work in a technological society.
- Learners need to have opportunities to structure their own understandings in self-directed learning contexts that empower them to be active knowledge builders.
- Students and citizens should be productive in terms of output.

As the same time Clements, Nastasi, and Swaminathan (1993) suggested that we were at a crossroads in terms of using computers in schools. They argued that schools could use computers either to reinforce traditional activities or, conversely, as an artifact of innovation. It would seem that we are still at that crossroads; recent calls to go "back to basics" (e.g., Donnelly 2006) might even indicate that we have done a U-turn. The paradox remains that even though there seems to be a consensus from all stakeholders that our education system is not delivering the skills that students need to function in the twenty-first century, there have been only a few examples of real commitments to reform and rethink education to ensure that such goals might be achieved. We will now turn to some examples where this has been attempted and achieved.

NEW LEARNING

In 2001 the Australian Council of Deans of Education, in an attempt to put education at the forefront of the federal election, presented the notion of "new learning" to suggest a new direction for education in the twenty-first century (ACDE 2001). New learning was conceptualized around eight propositions:

1. Education has a much larger role to play in creating society.
2. Learning will be lifelong and lifewide.
3. Education is one of the main ways to deliver the promise of democracy.
4. New basics are emerging.
5. Technology will become central to all learning.
6. The work of educators will be transformed.
7. The place of the public and private in education will be redefined.
8. The focus of education policy must change from public cost to public investment.

Three conditions—technology, commerce, and culture—are posited as shaping our lives and discussed in order to highlight the ways in which our world has fundamentally changed. Old learning was matched to the old world of work and characterized by syllabus documents that clearly laid out the scope of knowledge that needed to be mastered and sequences of skill acquisition. Textbooks coordinating with the sequence were the main resource for teachers. However, new learning recognizes that workers in the new millennium and beyond "require skills and sensibilities that are significantly different from those of the past" (ACDE 2001, 31). The argument for new learning is based on the fact that each aspect of the three conditions has changed, and education needs to change accordingly. For example, new technologies have reshaped the relationship between knowledge and the technological tools that we use. We need to be collaborative, multiskilled, and flexible so that we are able to extend our range of activities in order to solve problems and create new conditions for transformation. New economies and workplaces are places of diversity, and cultures of work are established yet continually evolving. Such activities are knowledge-based and don't rely on rote, mechanistic actions. This is a major change, and those who are able to make the transition will be the most effective knowledge workers of the twenty-first century.

In the context of their new learning charter, the "new basics" are a very different way of organizing knowledge. For example, mathematics is viewed as not "a set of correct answers but a method of reasoning, a way of figuring out a certain kind of system and structure in the world" (ACDE 2001, 89). This is particularly important because it suggests a new way of creating opportunities for students to become mathematical that is based in active learning, inquiry, and problem solving rather than on the memorization of facts and procedures that may or may not be used in authentic contexts. New learning requires that students be able to generate and pose their own problems so that they are able to solve them in a variety of ways with resources that are relevant. It may also require that they collaborate with each other and seek out professionals who may support them in their learning. With the advent of the Internet this assistance is more accessible. If resources or information is needed, the range of possible contact points has increased greatly because so many of them are online. Yet they require the machines and the know-how to use them effectively for specific purposes.

The curriculum framework of the new learning is based around three learning areas (see Table 2.1), which are mapped onto three domains of social action that "define the new person." This contrasts new learning with old learning and suggests the ways in which new citizens have to be flexible, curious, innovative, and imaginative to be productive and survive in the new era. These new technologies underpin the creation

Table 2.1 New Learning: New Worker, New Citizen, New Person

Learning Area	Work	Civics	Identity
Techne Technology, and more—the capacity to use various tools and instruments to get things done, technique, method, practical reasoning and science, human impacts on the environment	Scanning Discovery Innovation	Agency Selection Advocacy	Navigation Discernment Appropriation
Oeconomia Commerce, business, economics, and more—frameworks for getting things done in the social world, for being productive and effective, including work in the home and community as well as paid work	Calculation Entrepreneurship Innovation	Complexity Motivation Mediation	Negotiation Reflexivity Application
Humanitas Understanding one's own culture and the cultures of others, acting sociably, crossing boundaries, and working with diversity	Investigation Cooperation Reflection	Communication Ambiguity Compromise	Multiplicity Recognition Transformation

Source: ACDE 2001, 92.

of a new basics curriculum in schools and become important in the transformation of learning relationships both in school and in out-of-school contexts.

The organization of knowledge areas exemplifies the new ways of living in the twenty-first century. The three learning areas, given the Greek names *techne, oeconomia,* and *humanitas,* serve to illustrate the ways things can be done in a technological world; they also emphasize that these activities are carried out within the context of a social world characterized by commerce and business as well as in homes and communities. They also foreground the recognition that an understanding of diversity and culture ensures that we are able to work collaboratively and effectively in globalized economies and for the promotion of positive societal ideals.

The three domains of social action exemplify the nature of human activity in the areas of work, civics, and identity. The skills that individuals need for these contexts provide a stark contrast to those that were valued in old learning contexts. The three domains emphasize new skills that were previously not considered or had low status. In the past, for example, mechanistic actions and memorization of facts were elevated and regarded highly; application to real-world examples was not valued as highly as performance in school-based examination systems, which promoted the regurgitation of such facts.

Thus new learning provides a broad framework to consider the ways in which we might reconceptualize and organize knowledge for New Times. It also identifies the characteristics of the new citizen and the skills base required for people to function effectively in twenty-first-century society. Accordingly, drawing on Kalantzis and Cope (2005), we can say that new learning environments:

- Support a culture of innovation where risk taking is encouraged
- Provide contexts for collaborative learning
- Encourage problem posing and strategic thinking
- Establish learners as autonomous and outward-looking
- Promote higher-order thinking that draws from various knowledge bases and perspectives
- Cultivate a capacity for lifelong and lifewide learning
- Encourage sharing and communication of ideas using multimodal methods and the use of new technologies

NEW CURRICULA

At the systemic level there have also been a number of other initiatives to spur new ways of thinking about curricula in our schools, ones that complement the theoretical framework provided by new learning. In Queensland, Australia, for example, a new basics curriculum is supported by a productive pedagogies framework and rich task assessments. The consideration of curricula, pedagogies, and assessment in a simultaneous and complementary way is significant since it recognizes that the change process needs to include all aspects of teachers' professional work as well as promote new learning via a rethinking of traditional knowledge and subject matter.

Like new learning, the new basics curriculum (Department of Education, Queensland 2001) does not consider knowledge as residing in the traditional disciplines. However, rather than three organizational components, it has four:

- *Life pathways and social futures.* "Who am I and where am I going?"

- *Multiliteracies and communications media.* "How do I make sense and communicate with the world?"
- *Active citizenship.* "What are my rights and responsibilities in communities, cultures, and economies?"
- *Environments and technologies.* "How do I describe, analyze, and shape the world around me?"

The investigations and knowledge-building experiences that arise from the questions posed in each of the four areas can be initiated by the teacher or the students. The mode and means of inquiry are discussed, shared, and scaffolded in order to support optimal learning and knowledge building The Queensland new basics curriculum is supported by a productive pedagogies framework that consists of four basic areas:

- *Intellectual quality.* The goal is to ensure that students have opportunities to acquire and manipulate information and ideas in ways that transform their meaning and implications, understand that knowledge is not a fixed body of information, and can coherently communicate ideas, concepts, arguments, and explanations with rich detail.
- *Connectedness.* Here the goal is to provide students with experiences in which they can engage with real problems (whether practical or hypothetical) that connect to the world beyond the classroom, are not restricted by subject boundaries, and are linked to students' prior knowledge.
- *Supportive classroom environment.* This seeks to ensure that students influence the nature of the activities they undertake, engage seriously in their study, regulate their behavior, and know explicitly what they are being asked to achieve.
- *Recognition of difference.* The aim is for students to know about and value a range of cultures, create positive human relationships, respect individuals, and help to create a sense of community.

In each of these areas teachers can support and facilitate student investigations in specific and productive ways and mentor them about the ways in which they might organize their work and disseminate their findings.

The final aspect of the new curriculum in Queensland is rich task assessments that engage children in authentic activities that may (or may not) involve the use of new technologies (Department of Education, Queensland 2001). What distinguishes them from traditional assessment is that they are multifaceted and require an integration of knowledge and skills well beyond the simplistic type of knowledge and skill use that is assessed in computer-marked multiple-choice tests. Further, they do not have one right answer in the traditional sense, and might require working and collaborations in groups. For example, a rich task for children in grades 1 to 3 (age 6 to 8 years) is to create a multimedia presentation that encapsulates their investigation of an endangered plant or animal. The new basic referents for the rich task are:

- *Life pathways and social futures:* collaborating with peers and others
- *Multiliteracies and communication media:* blending traditional and new communications, mastering literacy and numeracy
- *Active citizenship:* interacting with local and global communities
- *Environments and technologies:* developing a scientific understanding of the world and building and sustaining environments

The targeted repertoires of practice are:

- Classifying ideas and information
- Collecting and collating data
- Comprehending the concept of ecological interrelatedness
- Comprehending the concept of environmental responsibility
- Dealing in an orderly manner with the parts of a complex whole
- Presenting a persuasive argument
- Respecting the integrity of primary evidence (and reporting data without bias or distortion)
- Setting out information in a cohesive report
- Structuring an argument
- Understanding the potential of media technologies (Department of Education, Queensland 2001, 5)

By outlining these criteria and describing the levels of achievement at which they are met, the assessment is specifically focused on the processes that are utilized during the course of the investigation and allows for a discussion and consideration of the type of knowledge that is generated in a context in which the learner has the opportunity to decide on the broad nature of the project and the ways in which it can be organized. What is also evident is that during the course of the investigation they are using knowledge across the disciplines and are required to engage with higher-order thinking skills in a rich way. Using new technologies is an essential part of this process, and children are afforded the opportunity to decide not only which media will support their inquiry but also how they will present their findings to their audience.

In reconceptualizing curricula, pedagogies, and assessment in this way, the focus for learning is knowledge building in communities of practices that support the communication of ideas in effective ways. As illustrated

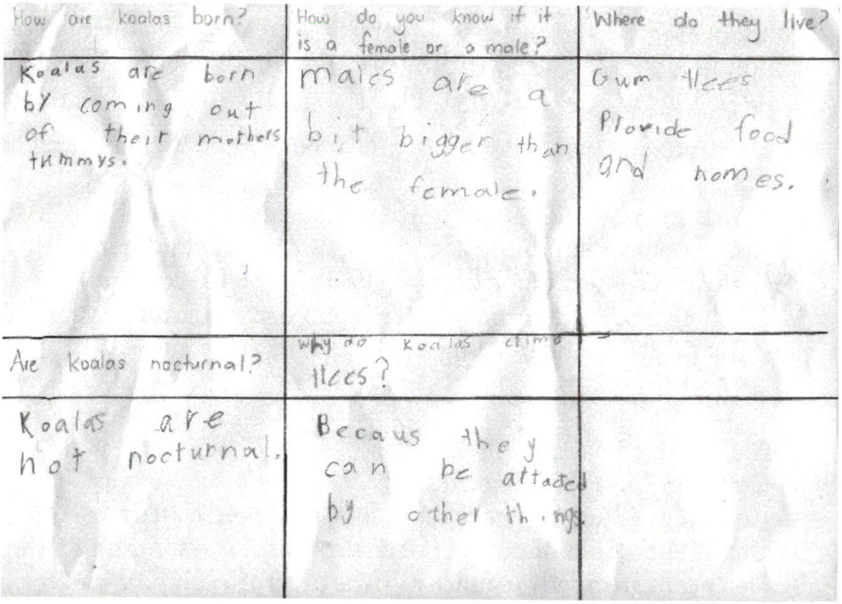

How are koalas born?	How do you know if it is a female or a male?	Where do they live?
Koalas are born by coming out of their mothers tummys.	males are a bit bigger than the female.	Gum trees Provide food and homes.
Are koalas nocturnal?	why do koalas climb trees?	
Koalas are not nocturnal.	Becaus they can be attaded by other things	

Figure 2.1 Finding out about koalas

above, such contexts also recognize the collaborative nature of learning and encourages teams of children to embark on investigations characterized by a desire to solve authentic problems as well as the goal of promoting and stimulating creative explorations of the children's life-worlds in order to consolidate and build new knowledge. Accordingly, learners are afforded opportunities to see themselves as instigators of investigations, using the skills they acquire in school to extend their capabilities in new and dynamic ways.

For example, in a project with early childhood teachers one of them described a learning experience that was initiated when a koala was sighted in the school grounds and the children went out excitedly to observe it.[1] On returning to the classroom the children wanted to find out more about koalas; some found books in the library, and one child decided he wanted to do his research on the Internet. Another student joined him, and after finding some relevant sources they created five questions for their research:

How are koalas born?
How do you tell if it is a male or female?
Where do they live?

Are koalas nocturnal animals?

Why do koalas climb trees?

The boys wrote these questions on a sheet of paper (see Figure 2.2) to support their further explorations on the Internet.

After this initial exploration the pair presented what they had found to the class, and they talked about the ways in which they could help koalas to live safely in proximity to humans. Another student suggested that they could make a poster to teach people how to look after koalas. During the next week the groundskeeper came to talk to the children about propagation, since the children had discovered that one of the main problems for koalas was finding enough food when trees were being cut down. She brought in a branch of eucalyptus and a box of seedling bags filled with soil. She explained the propagation process and then took the children outside to plant the seeds. Next the children were provided with the following scenario: *All of the eucalyptus trees have died. The koalas have nowhere to live. Design a machine that will propagate seeds into new eucalyptus trees.*

Two students created a design for a propagation machine with Kid Pix software and printed it out to share their design with the class.

Within such learning scenarios there are basic building blocks of skills and knowledge that are fundamental to being a capable and effective learner.

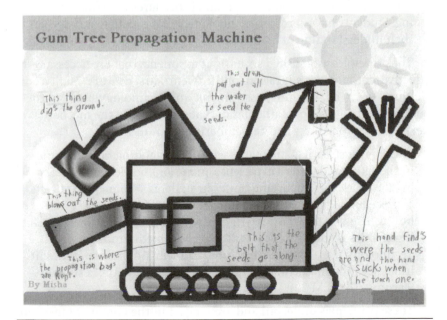

Figure 2.2 Designing for plant propagation

For example, students must be able to read, comprehend, and critique various types of texts, and must be fluent with numbers and patterns so that their use can support problem solving. Teachers of the twenty-first century are able to promote learning in environments in which children can acquire and use knowledge and skills to facilitate authentic investigations. This will enable their students to become effective citizens in a world that is rapidly changing and where the jobs that they will be doing may not have been invented yet. Reconceptualized curricula and a realization that we need to focus on new learning contexts support knowledge building and skill acquisition in school learning.

NEW STANDARDS FOR MATHEMATICS

At a different level, a professional organization, the National Council of Teachers of Mathematics, successfully reconceptualized the teaching of mathematics in the United States via stating new priorities for the subject, as exemplified in standards (e.g., NCTM 1989, 1998, 2000). The council, like the ACDE with its new learning charter, recognized that the teaching of mathematics needed to change dramatically in order to create a generation of learners that would be mathematically literate for the twenty-first century. They envisioned a mathematics curriculum that should be

> mathematically rich, providing students with opportunities to learn important mathematical concepts and procedures with understanding. Students have access to technologies that broaden and deepen their understanding of mathematics. (NCTM 2000, 1)

The principles established six basic components that are necessary for effective mathematics education for the twenty-first century: equity, curriculum, teaching, learning, assessment, and technology. Each of these contributes to a view of mathematics that goes beyond the mechanics of performing procedures and remembering formulas.

> Students must learn mathematics with understanding, actively building new knowledge from experience and prior knowledge. . . . Learning the "basics" is important; however, students who memorize facts or procedures without understanding them are often not sure when or how to use what they know. In contrast, conceptual understanding enables students to deal with novel problems and settings. . . . Technology is essential in teaching and learning mathematics; it influences the mathematics that is taught and enhances students' learning. (NCTM 2000, 5–6)

These principles underpin and are viewed in the context of five content areas (number, algebra, geometry, measurement, and data analysis and probability) and five process standards (problem solving, reasoning and proof, communication, connections, and representation) that together delineate the knowledge and skills considered to be fundamental to effective functioning in our data-drenched society.

As one example of the principles in action, a new set of curriculum materials, in which the use of new technologies such as computers and calculators was embedded, was produced in the United States under the title of Investigations in Number, Data, and Space. The series integrated computer and calculator activities as an intrinsic and integral part of mathematical investigations (Clements et al. 1995). In doing so, they helped to build the notion that new ways of thinking were supported by a variety of technological resources and required learners to think, solve problems, lead inquiries in appropriate ways, and communicate their ideas and findings to authentic audiences. A number of empirical studies in both the United States and Australia (e.g., Clements and Battista 1994; Clements et al. 1997; Yelland 1998, 1999, 2002a) have illustrated the ways in which this new curriculum provided contexts in which children could acquire the fundamental knowledge and skills required to support independent and collaborative investigations.

In several modules of the Turtle Paths curriculum (e.g., "How long, how far?") software called Geo-Logo (a variation of Logo) is incorporated to support the learning of geometric concepts (e.g., length and shape).[2] When Papert launched Logo, he conceptualized it as an environment or microworld in which children would be able to learn mathematics more effectively. Just as it was better to learn French by being in France, he asserted, it would be better to learn mathematics in mathland (Papert 1980).

He suggested that microworlds are very powerful environments for learning because they afford the opportunity for children to make sense of ideas in a context where true and false, right and wrong are not the decisive criteria. In a (computer) microworld learners are able to actively explore concepts in new and dynamic ways that would not have been possible without the technology, and in so doing construct knowledge that has meaning for them. Geo-Logo extends the potential of Logo. It is a computer environment in which commands are given to a turtle to instruct it to perform specified actions related to moving (forward and back) and turning (right and left). These are accompanied by numeric inputs that determine the extent of the movement. In addition, it has on-screen tools that assist children to plan and make decisions about what they want to do. For example, there is a ruler to help with quantifying distance, and turns can be measured with an on-screen protractor. Other features include animated rays to show the extent of turns and a replay or step function that allows children to review their actions prior to deciding what to do next. The Geo-Logo screen format allows children to type code in a window and watch the turtle follow each command as it is typed. Additionally, the "teach" tool can be selected to create a procedure once they are satisfied with the code that they have created. The aim of the Investigations in Number, Data, and Space curriculum is to promote and encourage active exploration and interrogation of concepts, and the Geo-Logo environment supports this way of working.

In one activity a group of eight-year-old children in a third-grade class worked on an activity called Geo-Face in which they designed a face in Geo-Logo. They wrote procedures for each part of the face (ears, eyes, mouth, and nose). They could choose what shape each part of the face might be; however, there had to be at least one of each shape, and the perimeter length of each part (nose 90, mouth 200, eyes 100, ears 120) was specified in the instructions for the activity. The final command for each procedure had to be "setheading 0" so that the turtle was facing the top of the computer screen.

The children demonstrated a high level of engagement with the activity at the planning and assembling stages of the task. Only one pair, Tim and Courtney, decided not to include a square in the final Geo-Face, even though a square mouth had been decided upon. When they entered the commands on the computer, they changed the mouth to a rectangle because they thought that the square did not "look right." They used rectangles to create the mouth, eyes, and ears and then developed a triangular nose. The other pairs of children tended to create shapes that were somewhat predetermined by the number assigned to the perimeter. For example, 100 and 120 can be easily divided into four equal parts of 25 or 30, respectively, and four sections can produce a square or rectangle.

Ryan and Adam seemed to be very protective of their ideas and opted to do their planning well away from the other groups so that no one could "steal" their ideas. When the other children came over to see what they were doing, as occurred often, Ryan and Adam covered up their work so that it could remain a mystery. However, they constantly wandered around the room to check on what everyone else was doing. In their planning Ryan and Adam decided that they wanted triangular eyes, and since the perimeter of each triangle had to be 100, they were forced to calculate the length of each side carefully. Ryan reasoned: "If it has to be 100 all the way around and the triangle has three [equal] sides, we need to have 100 divided by 3. Where is the calculator?" He entered 100 divided by 3 and exclaimed "Wow" when the answer 33.333333 appeared. He then asked if it was okay to use that number. He said that he knew the dot was a decimal and that the number was 33 but wondered if he had to type in all the other 3s as well. Even when he was advised that he need not do this, he decided that he would, and the command "FD 33.333333" was included in the final procedure. This process was obviously stimulating to the boys, since they were then keen to have another face part that included a decimal point. They reasoned that if the nose had to have a perimeter of 90 they could divide it by 4 to get an answer that would have a decimal point. Accordingly, his square nose had sides of 22.5. They seemed to be quite disappointed when they studied the task requirements for the remaining face parts and realized they could not use this technique again. It was apparent at this stage of the unit that Ryan and Adam had a good understanding not only of number in connection to the length of the sides of the shapes but also of the idea that turns for equilateral triangles were 120 degrees and those for rectangles and squares were 90 degrees. Each of the procedures that resulted in a face part ended with a turn so that the turtle was facing the top of the screen, as required. Additionally, as with all the student pairs, the triangle was drawn with the first command being "rt 30" so that it would be "straight."

In their completion of the Geo-Face the children revealed a deep understanding of number and its role in the development of component features that were planned, developed, and entered using Geo-Logo code. They used numbers and mathematical operations that were well beyond those expected of their grade in curriculum documents and more complex than any ideas that they had the opportunity to discuss in class.

As part of the curriculum the children also designed projects of their own, and as they did so it was apparent that they were:

- Analyzing geometric figures in order to determine their role/place in the final product
- Understanding that shapes can be moved to new locations and flipped and turned without losing their essential properties—that is, the angles in a square were always 90 degrees even when the square was tilted
- Using their mathematical knowledge, especially related to number and operating on numbers, to produce length and turns for different functions

At the planning stage a framework provided by the teacher proved to be particularly useful in assisting the children to organize their ideas in a coherent form. It also served the function of helping the children decide what constituted a reasonable project. At first they made elaborate drawings, apparently not recognizing how difficult they would be to develop as Geo-Logo projects. However, when they came to record their ideas as component parts and procedures, it became immediately apparent that the plans would have to be considerably modified in order to enter them as code. The pairs of students worked together over four sessions in order to produce their project pictures. The results, like those of the Geo-Face task, indicated a sound understanding of basic mathematical ideas together with a high level of skill in programming involving the development and combination of procedures.

In developing their house (Figure 2.3) Ryan and Adam decided that they needed to use a semicircle in order to put some domes on the roof section. After thinking for a while, they remembered that Angela and Denielle had incorporated a circle in one of their projects. They asked if they could go into the girls' file to "have a look at it." They found the procedure for the circle, copied it, and then relocated it in their own work file. When they used the circle for their chimney top, however, they realized that it was too large for their structure, so they modified it to

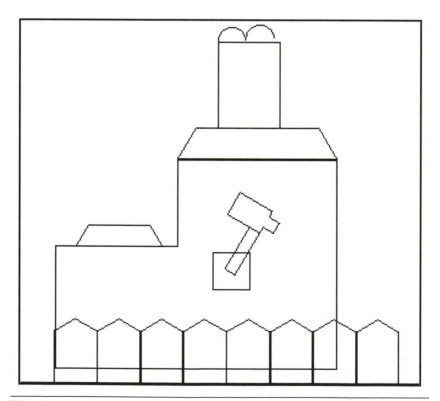

Figure 2.3 Security house

suit the size of their roof by increasing the size of the turns in the circle procedure.

The incident is interesting not only for the ingenuity of using the procedure that another pair developed but also because the logistics of entering, copying, and pasting files was done only as a management aid while the research was being conducted, yet the children had observed it and then used it when they needed to do so.

The house project also reveals the kind of detail that the children were able to develop in their drawings. The pair constructed the security camera very carefully using a top-down approach. They knew what they wanted the final product to look like, and so they planned and built it, moving from their ideas to paper and finally to the computer representation with Geo-Logo. Initially, the drawing of the camera was very complex. When we suggested that this would be difficult to draw on the computer, the boys made new plans that were much simpler and contained the basic shapes that they knew they could draw—a very practical approach. They then considered each shape separately and built up the camera before placing it on the house.

In the second year of this particular study the children went on to explore a variety of concepts within the Geo-Logo context. By the end of the research they were creating procedures with variables, using these to make patterns and pictures, using coordinates to position the turtle, and incorporating the use of negative numbers. In this way they were playing around with ideas that were well in advance of those expected in traditional educational settings, and the technological setting enabled them to do this in a nonthreatening and playful manner.

NEW LITERACIES

In another study we worked with early childhood teachers in order to facilitate a greater understanding of the ways in which they could support the children in their classes to become multiliterate in the twenty-first century.[2] The case for multiliteracies (New London Group 1996) was premised on the belief that a broader view of literacy beyond the traditional language based approaches was need. In the pedagogy of multiliteracies, modes of representation beyond the linguistic alone are significant; they include visual, audio, gestural, and spatial modes as well, and combinations of these. The New London Group contends that understanding and making meaning from multimodal texts is an essential component of being literate in contemporary times. They provide two examples. First, they argue that the mass media images that seem to permeate every aspect of our lives contain both linguistic and visual modes and that they

Table 2.2 A Pedagogy of Multiliteracies

Situated practice	Immersion in experience
Overt instruction	Systematic, analytic, and conscious understanding
Critical framing	Interpreting social and cultural contexts
Transformed practice	Transfer of meaning-making process

are linked for specific readings and purposes; magazines, for example, use significantly different grammars based on their social and cultural content. Second, they suggest that living in contemporary times means that everyday experiences such as a visit to the mall not only require an understanding of linguistic meanings in the form of written text but also include the multimodal aspects of the design of language, that is, an understanding of the spatial architecture of the buildings and a recognition of the impact and meaning of written signs, music, logos, and lighting.

[A]ll meaning-making is multimodal. All written text is also visually designed. Desktop publishing puts a new premium on visual design . . . spoken language is a matter of audio design as much as it is a matter of linguistic design understood as grammatical relationships. (New London Group 1996, 81)

The use and relevance of all the modes will vary with culture and context and are linked to pedagogical practices in which "language and other modes of meaning are dynamic representational resources, constantly being remade by their users as they work to achieve their various cultural purposes" (New London Group 1996, 64).

The pedagogy of multiliteracies is centered on four key principles of what a good teaching and learning environment should encompass. It maintains that teaching and learning about the design of meaning should include a mix of situated practice, overt instruction, critical framing, and transformed practice.

The data from our study confirmed that teachers still held traditional views of literacy that focused on print literacy, but they recognized that they could extend their pedagogical repertoire to support children to become multiliterate via the use of new media. In our conversations with them it was apparent that they realized not only that different modes of representation were possible but also how those might impact on learning by facilitating meaning making and self-esteem. For example, one teacher, Louise, reported:

I think giving them the independence to draw on these various technologies, they are able to draw on and express themselves in different ways that they may not get anywhere else. Like they may not get that opportunity anywhere else in their life to tell their story by using this form of technology. I just think that this might be empowering.

As a result of their participation as teacher-researchers in the project, they embarked on rethinking the nature of multiliteracies and were able to create contexts in which the children in their classes could utilize multimodal representation (linguistic, visual, audio, gestural, and spatial) to make meanings in new ways.

George the Builder[3]

Encouraged by his preschool teacher and his family, George, four years old, displayed an interest in block construction and building and had demonstrated a keen sense of spatial awareness from early in his preschool years. Spatial awareness, or being spatially intelligent, refers to being able to think and communicate effectively in the spatial domain (Diezmann and Watters 2000). Spatial skills such as map reading, drawing, building, representing, and creating models are now being recognized as playing an increasingly important role in becoming numerate and scientifically literate, especially with regard to using visually oriented new technologies (Diezmann and Watters 2000). The classroom climate supported George's constructions and investigations, with the preschool teacher exploring her own conceptions of how to transform her teaching from viewing her preschoolers as beginning literacy learners (often from the deficit view) to viewing the children as multiliterate and already demonstrating competencies and skills in different media. In the predominantly play-based preschool program, George had access to many play and learning areas, including construction materials, and opportunities to use various new technologies within his play and learning, such as documenting his preschool experiences using a digital camera (this involved the preschoolers uploading and saving their own photographs) and using various computer programs. In the preschool year, George was described by his teacher as having a clear vision for how his various constructions should look and definite ideas about how they should be constructed. Embracing George's self-efficacy in the area of building, planning, and construction work, George's preschool teacher, Louise, recognized and valued George's creative efforts: "It is this intricate work . . . his mind is just going all the time. Thinking about what he can do . . . [a]t home he has all the equipment available such as masking tape, etc., his mum has provided him." George's creativity was being supported at home, and he was encouraged to keep a journal with all his plans and drawings in it. His mother commented that George will "find anything and create."

The preschool teacher could see that George was active and keyed into exploring and building his visual literacy skills. In one preschool session George built a complex, very detailed raised railway station out of blocks. George had spent a long time constructing it when another child accidentally knocked it down. George was devastated, but he quickly recovered and explained to his teacher that he wanted to draw his construction so that he would not forget what it looked like. He proceeded to do so, spending most of the session making a detailed drawing of the lost construction. The teacher remarked that George's vision for building and designing was realistic and intricate and that he was spatially aware and talented. She commented that when his train station was knocked over and he said, "I know how to fix it. I need some paper to draw my design of the train set," she thought, "Wow, what quick thinking, and his working from a plan, his vision and his ideas made me realize that he has a lot more going on [inside]. He blows my mind. I think it was a surprise, just the idea of a plan." Later when George made another construction, digital photos became a record of what he had built, so he was able to reflect on what he had previously done as well as use his ever-increasing linguistic capacity to engage in discussion with Louise and others about the particular features of each construction.

In his next year of education, the first year of formal schooling, George (now five) had the opportunity to create a Lego animation with some peers. His teacher had brainstormed possible narrative ideas with the children, who were to create a short animation using Lego blocks to tell their story. George and his peers created "The Zoo," a three-minute animation using PowerPoint. Again George was able to explain the process they went through to create the animation, and it was evident that he was very proud of his own contribution of building the set and the characters.

As this short glimpse into George's early education suggests, the pedagogy used was shaped by the teachers' understandings of their students as literacy learners. In this case George's spatial literacy talents were recognized and supported over the course of two years by his teachers, who provided learning environments that were well resourced with new technologies (e.g., computers and digital cameras) as well as with traditional construction materials. This application of the pedagogy of multiliteracies involved three main processes: taking a broad view of the child as a competent learner (portrait), practicing a multiliteracies pedagogy (pedagogy), and conceptualizing multiliteracies pathways and providing extension experiences (pathways).

LEARNING FOR DESIGN

More recently, and as an extension of the pedagogy of multiliteracies, learning activities that exemplify pedagogy as knowing in action have become the focus of another project called Learning by Design, which posits four fundamental ways of knowing: experiencing, conceptualizing, analyzing, and applying (Kalantzis and Cope 2005).[4] (See Figure 2.4.)

Experiencing is regarded as immersion in the everyday lifeworld of the learner and involves the teacher in planning two different kinds of experiences for learners: the known and the new. In order for learning to be meaningful there needs to be a link between what is already known and what will be experienced. In experiencing the known, teachers afford opportunities for students to make links with their prior knowledge and experiences (e.g., personal, community) so that they are able to use it to make connections to the new learning that is planned.

Conceptualizing enables learners to make meaning from their experiences and build ideas or concepts about the nature of things and ideas and how the world works. In traditional curricula, the learning of abstract

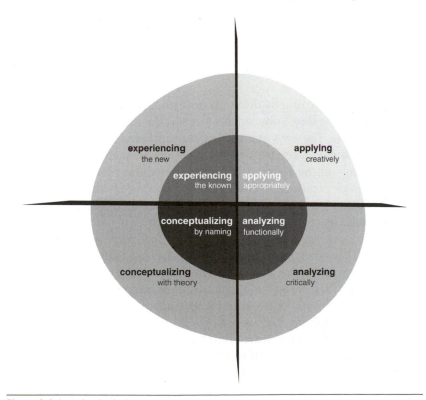

Figure 2.4 Learning by design

concepts is often the stated goal. By contrast, in learning by design, learners first name the specific ideas that they have encountered, and then expand the concept outward by generalizing to other situations. For example, a learner first recognizes and names a river and the parts that make up that specific river; next, the learner builds up a theory about what a river is and could build a model or diagram depicting the constituent parts of the whole.

The knowledge process of *analyzing* requires that learners be able to examine a context, event, or piece of information and be able to articulate in a systematic and critical way the underlying assumptions and implications of its application or function. In analyzing, learners consider what an idea means and how it might impact on themselves, the community, or the world. When critically analyzing knowledge, learners are required to ask questions about the ramifications of its application in diverse situations.

Finally, in *applying* what we know in diverse ways, especially in authentic contexts, we are extending learning so that it has a purpose and can add value to our lives and the lives of others. In applying appropriately, we often follow traditional ways of doing things, such as using objects for the purpose that they were designed. However, there are always opportunities to be creative by using things in innovative ways and creating contexts in which objects and ideas are redesigned or transformed.

The focus of learning by design is on meaning and action as ways of knowing, and the four knowledge processes described are the constituent parts of this. The ways of knowing are sensitive to cultures, learners, knowledge domains, and pedagogies, so they will have different emphases depending on the context they are planned for. Making the knowledge processes explicit enables teachers to consider which facets they regard as being most effective depending on their context and content. It also enables teachers to use these processes to support or scaffold students' deep learning. It is generally assumed that there is a link between pedagogical knowledge and learning outcomes (e.g., Darling-Hammond 2001). When working with teachers using the schema for their planning, we have noted that the essential conditions of learning—that is, belonging and transformation (Kalantzis and Cope 2005)—are usually met. Additionally, when the knowledge processes are made more explicit, it ensures that teachers and learners are fluent in their use, and this has a profound impact not only on learning outcomes but also on creating a positive classroom climate and helping students become confident lifelong learners.

RETHINKING ASSESSMENT

In rethinking learning in these ways it becomes apparent that traditional ways of measuring outcomes of learning also need to be reconsidered. At the current time it is inevitable that those responsible for the management of systems want simple forms of testing that typically have right and wrong answers that can be marked by a computer. Not only are these easily administered but they allow for immediate comparisons across school systems and age cohorts, enabling politicians and bureaucrats to claim that their policies are effective. Tests measure specific, and usually finite, bits of knowledge. Such knowledge is often deemed to be "basic" (e.g., knowing the sounds that the letter *c* can make in different words), "fundamental" (e.g., knowing how to add two numbers or recognize and name specific shapes), and "culturally essential" (e.g., knowing the dates of significant events in history, such as that World War II started Europe in 1939). The point is that those in control have decided that these bits of knowledge are important and need to be remembered and demonstrated in tests. Other tests (e.g., PISA) claim to afford opportunities for participants to demonstrate their problem-solving abilities. These tests are administered internationally and are often used as an indicator of the health of the education system. To be successful in tests, students must demonstrate their capacity to hold on to specific sets of knowledge and use them during the test period. There is no connection to any other application or context, but it is generally assumed that some of the knowledge will stay with them and be used again, or serve as a basic component on which other facts might be built.

More complex forms of assessment take time and often require more subjective criteria. In considering productive assessment and productive performance, Hayes and colleagues have suggested that assessment "needs to be rearticulated and pulled back into teachers' professional dialogue." They also argue that:

> the alignment of curriculum, pedagogies and assessment is central to the enhancement of teacher effects on student learning and indeed, when complemented by appropriate whole-school culture and leadership practices, necessary to enhancing whole-school effects so that schools can make a difference. (Hayes et al. 2006, 126)

Their notion of productive performance is related to the belief that pedagogies and assessment in schools need to be framed in the context of the stated intellectual and social outcomes that have been documented by schools and systems. There is an emphasis on depth of knowledge and the ability to apply it in various contexts. The communication of ideas articulately using a range of media provides contexts in which this might occur. The tasks used to evaluate productive performance have been designed as rich tasks: multidisciplinary, collaborative and/or individual, and sustainable over a period of time.

In one rich task the students were required to create travel itineraries for visitors to their town or another chosen location. The new basics referents for the tasks were:

- *Multiliteracies and communications media:* blending traditional and new communications media, communicating and using language, developing intercultural understandings, and mastering (aspects of) literacy and numeracy
- *Active citizenship*: operating within shifting cultural identities and understanding the historical foundations of the particular context under investigation

The targeted repertoires of practice were:

- Applying the techniques and procedures of mathematics to budgeting
- Generating graphical texts (e.g., maps, diagrams, charts, timelines, timetables)
- Interpreting information presented in a variety of formats
- Reassembling information presented in a variety of formats (e.g., text, movie, photographs)
- Influencing opinions via oral and or written presentations
- Understanding and appreciating the views of others and the context in which they live
- Using new technologies (e.g., the Internet, graphing software) to present information

The task is identified in such a way that the children are able to follow the task requirements but have enough leeway to choose the specific example they want to investigate. Ideas, hints, and comments can be provided by the teacher, while indicators of both acceptable and high-quality performance are provided and usually are discussed with the students prior to the start of the investigation so that they are able to understand the intended outcomes.

In this case high-quality performance was to be evidenced by:

- Deep understanding of one's local culture and/or another culture via the presentation of itineraries that foster a mutual appreciation of the culture and a recognition of the similarities and differences between them, as shown in the selection of places of interest

- Proficient communication of information (e.g., itineraries and costs) in appropriate formats so that details are clear and comprehensive
- Succinct and appropriate argumentation to justify all aspects of the presentation and decisions related to stated purpose and context

Acceptable performance was to be evidenced by:

- Travel itineraries that reflect the stated interest of the visitor
- Sufficient details regarding costs in a viable schedule that highlights significant places of interest.

Stating the criteria for outcomes is a significant and important part of the assessment process and represents significant work on the part of the teacher. It constitutes what Robinson (2005) has called the Michelin view of assessment, whereby, as with the famous restaurant review system, criteria at multiple levels are established and those who are under review have the opportunity to fulfill the criteria at various levels of attainment. It also enables a clear communication about the goals of the proposed work to learners, so that they are able to plan accordingly and decide how they can best meet the criteria at the level they choose. This contrasts to the McDonalds standardized approach, where the universal standard is stated and if you don't meet it you are deemed to be inadequate.

Teachers that I have worked with have indicated that the collaborative sharing of designing criteria for rich tasks was essential to the success of the process. Teachers in the state that initiated this new approach found the tasks and assessment guidelines were invigorating and provided a new catalyst for engagement in their classes. However, once the tasks were set up, the teachers also incorporated ideas about the assessment from the children after they had the opportunity to reflect on their own learning and discover what they valued in the experience.

In the Children of the New Millennium project one of the teachers incorporated the ideas in a different way and created electronic portfolios of learning. Since her class was of kindergartners (five years of age) she invited sixth graders (eleven-year-olds) to act as "buddies" to support the project, since they had the necessary technological and language expertise. This included being able to use digital video and still cameras, knowing how to use PowerPoint, and being able to construct simple and effective sentences to capture what the five-year-olds were describing as their learning in kindergarten.

Sean's portfolio (Figure 2.5) summarize his views on his first year at school:

I am a reader
I am a writer

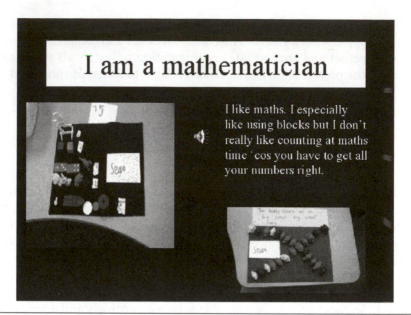

I like maths. I especially like using blocks but I don't really like counting at maths time 'cos you have to get all your numbers right.

Figure 2.5 "I am a mathematician"

I am a mathematician
I speak and listen
I am an artist
Playing helps me learn
I am fit and healthy
I choose my learning
I think about my learning

This form of documentation about individuals' learning goes beyond knowledge acquisition to facilitate their reflections about the experience of learning itself and enables them to build a strong identity of self as learners who are engaged and interested in the process. Having a permanent and electronic version of these experiences enables them to see their growth over time and becomes a powerful record of their progress, thus building their confidence and providing a catalyst for sharing their achievements with their families.

SUMMARY

This chapter has considered the nature of living in the twenty-first century and some ways in which systems (Departments of Education) and professional bodies (e.g., ACDE, NCTM) have begun the process of making curricula, pedagogies, and assessment relevant and meaningful for New Times. Examples from classrooms and children's work have illustrated the ways in which learning can embody these new conceptualizations about teaching and learning in the new century, not only to demonstrate the ways in which new technologies are relevant to this new learning but also to alleviate the fear of those who see traditional knowledge forms as being discarded or undervalued in new curricula. New learning exemplifies deep learning rather than superficial coverage of topics, and the depth of understandings about the world that we inhabit is evident in the children's own reflections about their personal learning experiences. For example, Sean stated at the end of his kindergarten year:

> I choose my learning and I choose to learn about life-guards and how to save people's lives if you go out of the flags. . . . It does not matter if you make a mistake because I know I am still learning and it is very fun and even if you make a mistake you still get to learn.

Today, to be well educated, citizens must be able to use the knowledge that they acquire in creative and flexible ways in order to generate new understandings. In reflecting on the history of innovation and change, it is apparent that new ideas and new ways of thinking and doing have been accompanied by new technologies, which change the very nature of the activities that we can participate in. Our education systems need to inculcate a culture of creativity and innovation so that we are able to keep up with the breathless pace of change in the world outside schools.

> The new technologies do not mean simply that we have new ways of doing things we did before: businesses, organisations and individuals everywhere are faced with entirely new forms of work, leisure and ways of being. We are trying to meet this new social and economic paradigm using the assumptions and preoccupations of the old intellectual paradigm of education. . . . The relationships between education and the world we actually live in are being stretched to breaking point. (Robinson 2001, 92–93)

The creative potential of children and adults can be harnessed in partnerships to challenge and create new contexts for engagement and learning so that we are able to move beyond the knowledge society to a creative one where education is serving the needs of the children who experience them.

NOTES

1. ARC Linkage Grant. Hill, Yelland, Mulhearn. "Children of the New Millennium," 2002–03.
2. ARC Linkage Grant. Lee, Yelland, Harrison. "A Pedagogy of Multiliteracies with ICT for Early Childhood Education," 2003–6.
3. This vignette was written by Anna Kildeny from the project notes and discussion with the teacher.
4. ARC Linkage Grant. Kalantzis, Yelland, Cope. "Learning by Design: Creating Pedagogical Contexts for Knowledge Building in the Twenty-first Century," 2006–8.

3

MAKING MEANING: TECHNOLOGY AS PLAY

In the first years of life, before school, children have a myriad of opportunities to learn in informal settings around their home and communities, and it has been widely recognized that these early years are of major importance in shaping behaviors and subsequent learning. This chapter examines learning through play, which is regarded as the main vehicle of learning in the early years, and contends that any consideration of play needs to incorporate the wide range of various modes of representation, dimensions, and contexts. These include technology as play, playing with ideas in multimodal ways, and storytelling as play. The role of the teacher in relation to each of these is described via the use of specific classroom-based examples.

PLAYING TO LEARN

In early childhood education the main forms of learning are regarded as being grounded in play. This belief is based on ideological, philosophical, and pedagogical principles arising out of the work of educators such as Montessori, Isaacs, Froebel, and Steiner. Later it became inextricably linked to the theory of Jean Piaget (e.g., Piaget 1972) and the belief that children learn when they are able to construct meaning from their experiences with the objects that they encounter. In Piaget's theory the young child is only capable of learning via sensory-motor experiences with objects; later the children become capable of making abstractions and formulating ideas and concepts based on these initial explorations. Not only is play thought to be the most vital aspect of learning, but it provides opportunities for young children to enhance their self-esteem and confidence, engage in collaborations that impact on their social skills, and make their own sense of the world that they inhabit; thus play contributes in a positive way to children's emotional development. Play is a fundamental component of early learning and the all-round development of the child in the formative years.

Traditionally, play is regarded as having particular characteristics. For example, Pellegrini (1991) considered play as consisting of three dimensions: disposition, context, and observable behavior. *Disposition* includes desire, attention, exploration, nonliteral behavior, variety, and active engagement. The *context* or setting of play is usually chosen by the child and tends to be informal. Pellegrini maintains that the *observable behavior* of play can be related to the three stages of play suggested by Piaget: functional, symbolic, and games with rules. Having defined these dimensions, Pellegrini contends that the more they are evident in the child's activity, the more playful the activity is. The idea that activity can be regarded as occurring on a continuum from play to nonplay is useful since worklike activity that might be initiated and scaffolded by a teacher usually contains playlike dispositions such as attention to the task and active engagement.

The notion that cognitive challenge, ranging from simple to complex, is inherent to play was suggested by Sylva, Roy, and Painter (1980). Complex play is characterized by the presence in observable behavior of thinking and problem-solving skills and the incorporation of materials and people in the play process. Complex play is regarded as high-yield in terms of providing opportunities for learning since it offered significant cognitive challenges within the context of child-defined goals and strategies to achieve those goals. In contrast, moderate- or low-yield (simple) play activities are not viewed as offering opportunities for planning, responding to feedback, and evaluating the progress of the activity.

The role of the teacher in play has been the source of much discussion. Froebel supported an informally structured approach, while Montessori preferred more formal sessions with carefully selected materials designed to promote specific aspects of child development. Both Froebel and Montessori schools are grounded in the belief that self-directed activity and engagement (intrinsic motivation) are essential components of effective learning environments, but teacher interaction with children is also vital if learning is to occur. Later, Piaget's theory contended that children could learn only when they were able to actively construct their own knowledge, which suggested that the role of the teacher was limited. Further research (e.g., Meadows and Cashdan 1988) has shown that rethinking the role of play is needed, since important conditions for learning are not always evident in play scenarios. Meadows and Cashdan suggested three such conditions: sustained conversations with an adult, high complexity of play activities, and lively, purposeful involvement leading to creative discoveries. This led to social constructivist approaches in which teachers (or other adults) scaffold children in order to support learning in a reciprocal relationship so that they will ultimately adopt the strategies used and in turn become autonomous and self-initiated learners. This is compatible with the theory of Vygotsky (1978), who contended that children learn most effectively in their zone of proximal development (ZPD), which he viewed as being between what they can achieve independently and what they can do with the support of an adult or more knowledgeable peer. Vygotsky regarded play as a major component for leading development in the early years, but he maintained that the social contexts inherent in the planned interactions with more knowledgeable others enabled learners to make sense of ideas and create meanings more effectively. In this way play facilitates learning since it allows children to explore and take risks within the ZPD, where they can be extended in their thinking and achieve higher-level outcomes when guided.

It is thus apparent that the links between play being regarded as the main vehicle for learning and the pedagogies that are adopted in early childhood classrooms are complex and will depend on the philosophy and beliefs of the teacher and the system in which the teacher is working. There would seem to be an increased focus on specifying learning outcomes for young children as they enter schools, which has led many teachers to complain about the increased pressure for academic-type work activities in early childhood classrooms. Yet the belief that the best conditions for learning are found where there is active learning, inquiry, and problem solving, whereby children are engaged and curious in their explorations, permeates much of the work of early childhood educators and remains essential to planning for curricula and pedagogies in this phase of education.

However, this belief has been accompanied by the view that such explorations should be confined to the child's real world, using three-dimensional objects. Consequently, new technologies, particularly computers and television, are often seen as the antithesis to such activity, since they are thought to detract from real life and objects and require a high level of abstraction. Certainly, the nature of the concept of "toy" has changed considerably over the last decade, with the advent of new technologies that have had the effect of bringing additional dimensions to objects that had previously been relegated to a relatively passive role in interactions with their owners—now dolls can communicate their emotions, and new electronic devices have more appeal than many traditional objects that are simply made of basic materials. As Papert suggested, "Our concern must be to ensure that what is good about play is at least preserved (and hopefully enhanced) as the concept of 'toy' inevitably changes" (1996, 188).

In this environment there has been a burgeoning interest in toys that are referred to as "educational." This relatively new marketing strategy of labeling toys as educational would seemed to be aimed at parents who, in having to choose from a large array of toys, select ones that they hope are going to enable their offspring to learn more readily, and ultimately get an edge on other children who don't have such opportunities (A. C. Nielsen 2005). Adjectives such as "plush" are also now attributed to dolls, soft toy animals, and other toy objects, in what seems to be a method of making them appear more sophisticated and desirable. Yet even these toys need to have an educational perspective to make them attractive to parents and others who want to ensure that their kids lead in the competitive world. Coupled with this are recent advances in the electronics industry, which mean that most toys today have an electronic component. Thus, any consideration of play in the early years should consider the role of technology in play.

Plowman and Stephen described the use of ICT in preschool contexts and found that "children's interactions with the computer were frequently referred to, by adults and children, as 'playing with the computer' in the same way as they would talk about playing with the bricks or the model animals" (2005, 149). Consequently, computer use, with associated game play, was included in programs as part of the free play activity time. However, Plowman and Stephen found that while free play time was characteristically a time when there was minimal adult intervention, this was often not the case when the computer play was involved.

Plowman and Stephen identified three broad categories of adult involvement in computer play in the preschool setting: reactive supervision, guided interaction, and a hybrid approach that incorporated elements of each. The researchers found that in computer play scenarios *reactive supervision* was most common and operated by default rather than as a planned pedagogy; when on the computer, children rarely sought out assistance unless it was regarding turn taking or technical difficulties. They reported that *guided interaction* was useful in eliciting specific responses from children playing on computers and also (for practical reasons) in terms of assisting children how to play a game initially. Because it was time-intensive and because teachers often felt that it, like the *hybrid* approach, was the antithesis of free play, they would not adopt specific procedures that might have facilitated the sessions when the children were playing on the computer. However, teachers recognized that guided interactions with children while they were playing had the potential not only for eliciting information about what the children were doing on the computers but also for building on the concepts that were inherent to the software being used. The teachers in the study felt that they needed professional learning to support the development of pedagogical strategies around effective guided interactions on the computer. In the meantime, computer use in the preschool setting was regarded as being somewhat mundane due to the limited capacity of the early childhood software that was available. The titles were often drill and practice examples, which were entertaining for short periods of time but were not thought to have a great deal of learning potential built into them. Plowman and Stephen concluded that there was a need for:

> a more developed pedagogy for the use of computers in the playroom . . . for practitioners to have opportunities to become more familiar with the software available and to be encouraged to be more critical about whether or not the learning model inherent in software matches their own models of learning and the needs of the children. (2005, 153)

PLAYING WITH TOYS

The U.S. toy industry generated $20.1 billion of revenue in 2004 (Toy Industry Association 2004). This figure does not include video games, which accounted for a further $9.9 billion. It is thought that parents purchase toys they think will help their children to learn, and even believe that some toys will increase their children's IQ (A. C. Nielsen 2005). Accordingly, the range of toys marketed as being "educational" is ever increasing, as previously noted, and with the advent of new technologies toys are becoming increasingly electronic and sophisticated. Some (e.g., Cross 2004) have lamented that toys and the act of playing have become too high-tech, yet the range of possibilities for fun as well as learning is probably greater than it has ever been before, despite the fact that it may be much harder to navigate through the cornucopia of playthings available on the market and advertised with blitzkrieg regularity in all forms of media. Papert (1996) predicts that social toys will develop in many directions, one of which will be the creation of "digital dolls" that have all the characteristics of conventional dolls but exist only as bits in a computer.

The marketing of toys seems to be aimed at encouraging parents to believe in their educational power to give their kids a good start for learning. In this way, if they purchase the products for their children, not only can they be regarded as good parents but also their children will, as a result of playing with the toys, have an added advantage compared to those who don't. For example, in 2005 the Web site of a popular toy maker, Fisher-Price, suggested that "play brings out baby's potential."

> Even young infants are capable of exploring the world through play. Hidden in each experience is a thoughtful lesson that helps baby learn and grow. Provide baby with interesting things to look at and play with. Watch her thrive as she explores, discovers and develops new skills—and gains a passion for learning that will last a lifetime.

More specifically, the Web site provided advice about how to use the toys:

- Stimulate your newborn's visual skills with bold, simple patterns and bright, contrasting colors.
- Because baby listens and responds to your voice, point out toy parts and actions and describe them.
- Toys that are visually interesting and have different textures and activities help baby explore and encourage early thinking skills.
- Tummy time play is very important, helping baby develop arm and neck strength while gaining a different perspective.

Papert himself was involved in the creation of software called My Make Believe Castle, based on the notion that children can play or interact with digital dolls that exist in a mythical computer microworld. The software contains all the basic elements of traditional play scenes, such as the medieval castle complete with prince, princess, knight, and wizard. A witch can be sent wandering in the forest looking for basic ingredients for her spell while the prince looks on and then goes riding back to his home. These "dolls" can assume identities as defined by the players but are different from dolls made of atoms, yet they are still toys because they assume the functions of traditional toys. Papert (1996) envisaged a more dynamic role for such toys in which they are able to assume personalities that are defined by the user rather than at the production level; further, such toys could be transported by the child to a wide variety of digital worlds where the child could embark on new adventures, take risks, and create new identities and stories that stimulate, excite, and promote learning in a different dimension. These type of features are also found in successful video games, which enable children to assume or create identities of their choosing and embark on scenarios formed according to specific actions or decisions that they make. This can be very empowering for learners since it enables them to be confident and adventurous in their explorations, and it often provides contexts in which they are able to learn and share their discoveries with other learners.

For young children the linking of three-dimensional playthings or television or movie characters with computer software provides a valuable context for learning that should not be underestimated. For example, Fisher-Price has released CD-ROMs such as Discovery Airport, My Very First Farm, and Ready for School Toddler, which build on their three-dimensional dolls or figures that have been popular for some time. The activities that the digital dolls can participate in on the CD-ROM can be selected by the child playing with them, but what is often missing is the feature of play discussed at the start of this chapter, that is, the support of adults in extending the concept building or language of the context. In a similar way linking characters from Sesame Street with books, dolls, and computer software provides opportunities for adults to scaffold children's learning and help them to make connections between the media and create new meanings from each. There are excellent opportunities for links to be made between the three-dimensional medium of the real-world dolls and the virtual world of the computer, in which dolls can be played with in different ways. Understanding the properties of both types of dolls will assist children to understand the nature of each medium and how they can interact with the characters in each. Inherent to this are the knowledge processes that constitute Learning by Design, which were described in the previous chapter. For example, in playing in both mediums the child can conceptualize by naming and will be able to make generalizations and theorize about the ideas encountered.

The challenge for toy makers today would seem to be related to designing objects and environments so that children are able to explore ideas and meaning in their play-based activities. The manufacture of stand-alone interactive toys—that is, those with computer chips embedded in them—has increased rapidly. In 2000 they represented 60 percent of the new-toy market compared to 10.3 percent in 1997, and the figure has increased since that time. However, these new toys might be successful for the same reason toys have always been successful—the attachment phenomenon, which has kept the teddy bear popular for a long period of time. Still, toys that respond as the child's mood changes would seem to have a powerful potential to be long-lasting. Imagine a doll or bear that a child could tell stories to and have them recorded. The child would then be able to play them back at any time, which would appeal in terms of nostalgia and memory narratives. There is now the potential to extend the capacity of such toys so that they build on children's vivid imagination and allow them to explore the world in ways that were not previously possible.

Some toys are frequently marketed as being interactive when in fact they simply have a prerecorded voice that is not able to respond to the nuances required for meaningful interactions with young children. This is where parents and other adults can add value to the play of young children by interacting with them utilizing language (e.g., by questioning) and stimulating them to make new inquiries. Toys then become artifacts of learning that can promote meaning making and also contribute to increasing the social and intellectual capacity of the child in a positive way. Digital toys have the potential to extend such interactions in ways that were not previously possible, and some may also be linked to computers to expand this capacity. Luckin and colleagues, though, concluded that "the toys as they stand are not impressive learning partners. . . . However, the technology has potential . . . when the toy is present, children interact with their peer companion in the dyads and with the researcher in both dyad and individual situations" (2003,14).

A good example of the ways in which toys have evolved in their use of new technologies is Learn Baby Tad (see Figure 3.1). This product is described on the LeapFrog Web site by the maker as follows:

Figure 3.1 Baby Tad

Babies squeeze the sun on the daytime hand to hear six happy, active songs and to play a fun learning game—flashing lights follow the beat and guide babies to the color and shape buttons on Baby Tad's chest. And this adorable friend's cheerful encouragement and cute laugh make learning a delight.

When it's time for bed or for a long trip, your baby just squeezes the moon on the nighttime hand to play up to six minutes of uninterrupted classical music. This music soothes even the most active toddlers.

The Hug & Learn Baby Tad Plush introduces shapes, colors and learning songs.

Use the Learning Guide card to the right to find out more about the general categories of learning for the Hug & Learn® Baby Tad™ Plush. By clicking a category on the Learning Guide card, you'll see a list of knowledge areas that children develop when they play with this product and the skills on which those knowledge areas are based.

Thus the soft toy has morphed into the plush toy that has various features that can stimulate activity if supported by an adult or sibling who is capable of following the instructions. This is an important point since the technology is not intended to supplant interaction with others or simply add sounds to the play experience; rather, it can be viewed as a catalyst for activities. Parents and others can, for example, sing along with the songs, as well as use the toy to support the introduction of the language of colors or shapes, which is an intrinsic part of our daily lives. Further, this toy is part of a family of toys, and the character appears with them in books as well as in the electronic LeapPad book device, which aims to support early reading. This might be regarded as shrewd marketing to ensnare potential customers, but it has the advantage of providing a context for early learning, with the continuity of the character being adapted to various modes of learning that should ultimately benefit the learning experiences of the child if they are supported with effective scaffolding by adults or older children.

Digital television is set to have a large impact on the ways in which children experience and are able to interact with new media. For example, Actimates Barney is a plush toy that takes instructions from the TV program *Barney and Friends* and enables the child to participate in singing and dancing alongside the main character during the show. The toy not only requests the child to perform actions and songs but is also able to encourage her to "Watch this!" or ask questions like "What do you think will happen next?" during the course of the program. In fact, Strommen and Alexander (1999) have reported that children with such interactive toys are more active in watching the programs than those who do not have the toy: the presence of the interactive Barney or Teletubbies encourages more dancing and both verbal and nonverbal actions from the children.

PLAYING WITH WORDS AND STORIES

Young children love to hear, make, and read stories. In the previous section I emphasized how important it is for adults to interact with children as they are playing so that these contexts become opportunities not only to learn about ideas but also to build a vocabulary that can be used to make, retell and listen to narratives in whatever mode they are experienced. Preschool children can be encouraged to share their stories in a variety of forms in order that they have opportunities to extend their language use in different ways. This will provide them with contexts to build their vocabulary so that they are able to communicate with others and express their ideas effectively. Good preschool teachers do this as a natural part of their daily interactions with the children in their care. If a child does a drawing or painting, the teacher might ask the child to say something about it and often will write it as a sentence on the picture. Beginning in kindergarten, children take on the responsibility for the writing, as it is viewed as an essential skill to be acquired beginning right at the start of the education journey. However, the nature and extent of the stories created at this stage are usually limited not by the child's ideas and oral language but rather by the child's ability to be able to write them down so that the meaning can be understood by others. Becoming skilled in the writing process is long and arduous and takes many years to master. In the meantime, oral stories created by the children are much more complex and intricate than their written ones but often are lost since there is usually no permanent record of them unless one is synthesized by the teacher in her daily observation notes.

However, new technologies have the potential to impact on this learning in significant ways. First, they can provide contexts in which oral stories can be recorded and saved, and second, they can act as a stimulus to encourage oracy in the early childhood years.

One piece of software that affords the opportunity for children to share their stories with a wider audience and thus enrich their storytelling experiences is Kid Pix. The Kid Pix software is, at its most basic, an electronic art package. Children can create pictures using electronic utensils such as paintbrushes and pencils and are also able to use premade features such as shapes and stamps of everyday items (e.g., trees, animals, flowers). They

Figure 3.2 The toe monster

can import scanned pictures or photographs and digitally enhance them using the inbuilt drawing utensils. There is also a part of the program called Slideshow that enables a sequence of pictures to be viewed with a voice input. The Slideshow feature can be used for any type of presentation, from the simple to the sophisticated, depending on the aims of the user. For four-year-old storytellers it holds a lot of potential. Instead of stories that span one sentence, due to their limited capacity in their writing, children are able to have a permanent record of more sophisticated narratives collated with illustrations to form an electronic slide show or e-book. In one example, a four-year-old preschool child created the story of the Toe Monster accompanied by the following illustrated narrative:

One day a monster lived under my bed
He said "Unga bunga I'm going to eat your toes."
He was a toe monster
I said "Ha Ha I'm not afraid of you."
And he went away
Now he lives under my little brother's bed!

In another preschool setting the teacher, Harriet, wanted to create contexts for Frances, a mildly autistic child, to verbalize. This was extremely difficult, as Frances needed a lot of prompting to verbalize even when she had completed something that she seemed to be very proud of. When the teacher would say something like "This is a great drawing. What did you do here?" the child would not offer any ideas. Frances rarely offered information verbally even with subsequent follow-up directed questions such as "What color are the lines?" However, after playing around with Kid Pix for a while, one day she spontaneously came up to the teacher's aide and said: "Here is my tiger." She then followed it up with "Here is the tail. You can see it." The teacher noted in her reflective journal:

> For F to use that much language, is amazing . . . and to actually add on to the initial declaration with more information about the drawing was a first. Usually she waits for you. But now her own creativity and use of language was there. . . . I will give her more prompts and I know now [to let] her explore more. I feel that she is becoming more proficient.

Obviously the introduction of Kid Pix software had resonated with Frances, and she wanted to play with it a lot. She loved making random sounds with the stamps and the erasing feature, which made a sound like exploding dynamite.

On another occasion Harriet read the story of Goldilocks to the group, and many of them incorporated aspects of the story into their play in the following days. Frances played with the Goldilocks doll without verbalizing, and Harriet introduced the digital camera to her and showed her how to take a photo of the doll. She gave the camera to Frances and left her to play with it for the rest of the session. The next day Frances returned to playing with Goldilocks and asked for the camera again. Harriet was once more amazed, since by the end of the session Frances had produced a series of three photographs and told her that it was Goldilocks coming to the house, sitting at the table to eat the porridge, and then falling asleep—a huge leap in the use of oral language from a child who previously had been virtually silent. The use of the software and later the camera provided a learning environment that resonated with her and stimulated her to communicate with her teachers, who subsequently extended the experiences so that she was able to build up her vocabulary and capacity to communicate with others.

These learning scenarios serve to illustrate the ways in which new technologies provided a medium through which children can articulate well-crafted and interesting oral narratives and how they can be saved instead of being evanescent. Such types of activity seem likely to complement traditional storytelling in preschool and school settings and also enhance it, since the activities enable the children to use their imagination freely. It is hoped that they will enable children to build on them as their written skills advance.

PLAYING WITH IDEAS

In formal learning (e.g., preschool and school) contexts, especially in the early years, teachers have tried to incorporate learning via play with the everyday practical demands that systems and parents require in terms of providing opportunities for young children to become literate and numerate. Curricula such as the Investigations in Number, Data, and Space mathematics program, mentioned in Chapter 2, were created in the belief that young children should participate in activities that will enable them to make meaning and build knowledge in an environment where they are active explorers. It has always been contended that we need "concrete materials" or manipulatives to support this early learning. In a similar way to the discussion on play, what we now consider as a manipulative is under scrutiny. As Clements and McMillen have stated, "What is concrete to the child may have more to do with what is meaningful and manipulable than with its physical nature" (1996, 273).

Clements (1999) has also highlighted the unique characteristics of computer manipulatives and suggested that they include:

- Flexibility
- The ability to change arrangements or representations
- The storage and availability of configurations
- Recording and replaying children's actions
- Linking the concrete and the symbolic and providing feedback
- Dynamic linking of multiple representations
- Focusing the children's attention and increasing motivation

When learning in an investigative curriculum context with embedded technologies, children are able to play with and actively experiment with measures of length and angle in dynamic ways that were not previously possible. Yelland (2002c) found that in such contexts children could create understandings about measurement that were built up over time and that reflected the recognition of the need for consistency in units of measurement as well as an ability to estimate and modify quantities of measure to match varying scenarios. As an example, in one curriculum unit there was the opportunity to play a game in which children could compare the differences in measure of a given distance with varying "step sizes." That is, two turtles needed to move the same distance to an object, but one turtle's step size was larger than another. The children could successfully complete the activities without making the requisite connections between number and distance, but when scaffolded by the teacher they were able to articulate sophisticated levels of reasoning that illustrated that they were cognizant of the relationship between unit size and measurement. In the last in a series of four tasks, Jesse (age seven) was able to predict the measure for a given distance on the basis of his previous experience in the environment. He was trying to figure out how to traverse the distance between two points by comparing steps that were three times bigger than those of his original turtle, who had walked the distance with eight of its steps. His realization that the numbers could be connected by a factor of three was sudden and dramatic:

Jesse: Because see every step is three times bigger and it equals three . . . so and ours is three of little ones, that's how, that's how I was working it out.

Teacher: So for every step . . .

Jesse: Eight times three.

Teacher: So for every step, there's three little ones in it.

Jesse: So I reckon it's twenty-eight.

Teacher: So how could you do it on the calculator?

Jesse: Three times eight.

Teacher: Okay, do you want to try that, Jesse?

Girl: Three times eight [pause] . . . twenty-four . . . he said twenty-eight!

The geometric setting, with the turtle acting as "an object to think with," provided both context and reason for thinking about number and operating with them. The motivations included game settings and the desire to traverse a specific space. The models included length and rotation as settings for building a strong sense of both number and operations with numbers, with measuring and labeling tools to support this construction. The dynamic links between the two domains of symbolic text and graphics structured in the environment (e.g., a change in code is automatically reflected in a corresponding change in the geometric figure) facilitated the children's construction of the connections between their own number and spatial schemes. Finally, the environment provided feedback, so the children could reflect on their own thinking and could then articulate this clearly (Yelland 2002a).

SUMMARY

This chapter has provided examples of ways that we might extend contexts for play so that young children are exposed to different modes of representations, which in turn afford them the opportunity to formulate new understandings about their world and make meanings about ideas and concepts on the basis of their experiences.

The challenge for parents and educators is to maintain a balance between real-world (3-D) toys, which may have an electronic component, and the newer digital ones, which are screen-based. Clearly there is a space at the moment to include both in play opportunities for young children. The aspects of screen-based digital toys that make them more attractive is that they have the potential to broaden the range of play experiences by acting as a catalyst for interactions either with another child or with adults and by enabling children to make connections between representations that should enable them to derive greater understandings about concepts they are encountering during their play.

Certainly, children should have a variety of experiences as well as materials to support their play. Often it would seem that parents think that because they have purchased a toy or software their child will spontaneously want to play with it without adult intervention. This may be the case and can be appropriate, but it is also evident that these are learning moments in which parents or other adults can interact with the child with a variety of positive outcomes emanating from the conversations. For example, an adult can provide the context to broaden the language base of the child as well as ask probing questions that will facilitate the learning of specific concepts and, one hopes, enable them to make the appropriate abstractions that lead to higher levels of thinking and knowing.

Children's play with electronic toys will continue to grow, and the children will bring these experiences to school. This will impact on the ways in which they will want to play and use what is available in the center or classroom, and educators should take this into consideration when planning learning activities. The resources and playthings that children have prior to coming to school and in after-school activities are becoming increasingly influential in shaping what they are able to do. As these become more sophisticated, the gap between what is available in school and what can be found out of it is widening, and schools are in danger of being viewed as irrelevant if they don't match the expectations of the children who attend them. The following chapter will extend this discussion by considering informal learning in out-of-school contexts that have been established for children in low-socioeconomic-status areas, so that they are able to use new technologies for a variety of purposes. Additionally, it will build on the work of Moll and colleagues (1992), which contends that we need to consider and understand these and other out-of-school experiences and the subsequent impact on learning in order to link them effectively with in school experiences.

4

THINKING AND KNOWING:
INFORMAL LEARNING AT HOME
AND IN COMMUNITIES

What's the difference beween school and prison? At school you don't get cable TV.

—Chicago Tribune *columnist Steve Chapman*

LEARNING LIFEWORLDS

It is evident that children learn in a variety of contexts that include not just school but also their homes, their community, and beyond, incorporating both geographically distant sites and virtual locations. These contexts can be regarded as the lifeworlds of the learner (Cope and Kalantzis 2000) and constitute the "place of belonging" from which the learner is able to explore and expand the boundaries of experiences and learning. In this way learning involves broadening the lifeworld of experience with the support of more experienced others who are able to encourage risk taking and assist the learner to build connections to what is already known.

CONNECTING HOME AND SCHOOL

The work of Moll and his colleagues (1992) has involved teachers visiting the homes and communities of the children in their care in order to gather data on community "funds of knowledge," which were then used to build curricula responsive to local knowledge. This process is important since it connects learning in out-of-school contexts to what goes on in the classroom and recognizes the importance of the former in making a contribution to school learning. Teachers have found this to be a valuable source of information when it comes to understanding all aspects of the lives of children who inhabit their classrooms. In the Children of the New Millennium project we asked teachers to arrange home visits so that the children could take them on a "techno tour" of their house. The idea was that this would enable teachers to build a pedagogy using information from the home and community as well as being based in educational theory and practice. We hoped that the information gleaned in the techno tour would enable the teachers to make connections between school literacy and numeracy and the use of ICT in the home. It was designed not simply as a count of what types of technology were available in the home but also so that we might discover who used them and for what purpose. Since the teachers had not experienced this type of activity prior to their participation in the study, they asked for a framework that would guide their interactions during the tour. This is provided in Appendix 1, and it can be seen that the teachers wanted to agree on a broad conceptualization of what constituted ICT before they described the practical details of location, perceptions of ownership, and how the child was able to operate the particular example of ICT that was being shown. The teachers documented their techno tour in a variety of ways, from written narratives to PowerPoint presentations and edited video vignettes. When the teachers came back to the research circle it was apparent that this experience had been a valuable one that informed their teaching significantly. As one teacher, Sally, noted in her final report:

> The knowledge that today's children are bringing from home is increasing as more and more homes invest in the ICT tools that are fast becoming an integral part of our society. . . . We must be careful that our education system doesn't become outdated for the children that we are now trying to teach.

The techno tour had provided a useful context from which the teachers could use the information for planning effective learning experiences. For example, one teacher reported:

> The home visits and techno tour was enlightening in that they made me more aware of the range of skills the students already had in using ICT prior to school entry. Previously I expected that I would be exposing the students to opportunities for learning through the use of ICT for the first time, believing that most of their prior experiences would be for recreational use. . . . I have now redesigned my approach to working with new students in light of my research.

Another teacher of five-year-old children indicated that the techno tour had:

> Showed many things children could do on computers and Play-Stations that we didn't realise they were capable of doing or being exposed to. [They showed] a variety of interests, maturity and ability. . . . One example was N playing Age of Empires with his father on the computer together. N and his father collaborated, organised, made decisions, and constructed empires together. . . . The ICT skills that the focus children are using at home were not being used at school in a big way. . . . As educators we can no longer think about whether to use ICT in our classrooms, but how to use them to enhance key skills and attitudes in our children in all areas of the curriculum.

Additionally, the study of which the techno tour was a part had an important impact on the lives and practices of the teachers involved, as one indicated:

> Being involved in the project has made me aware of the need for constant awareness of and critical reflection about the use of ICT in the development of productive pedagogy. I will continue to ask children what they are learning; to gather data and reflect on who is using the technology and for what purposes; to explore the impact of gender and power and continue to explore how traditional and digital resources can combine to support the learning styles and development of all students.

In visiting the home of her student, a teacher, Monica, noted that the child's home had a variety of ICT that the child used. For example, Julie (age five) showed her the digital camera that her family had and was able not only to use it effectively but also to articulate the function and purposes of the camera:

> It's a digital [video] camera. My mum won it in a competition. [She proceeded to explain how it worked.] When you take a picture you open that . . . like this [she pointed to the lens cover and opened it] and you can shut it like that and when you want to see the photo you have taken you can look on that bit [she pointed to the screen]. It's connected to the PowerPoint, so it might be recording. [She indicates a digital camera that is not a video camera.] This is a digital camera too! There's a flashing light and when you look through the flash comes and you see some people. They keep the photos in there [on the camera].

As a consequence of her observations of Julie in her home, Monica used the Essential Learning Framework planning tool (http://www.sacsa.sa.edu.au/index_fsrc.asp?t=EL) to help her determine where she should go next with Julie's learning. Building on her observations of Julie at home, she decided on the following:

> Digital photos—explore the use of Julie taking her own photos in the school context and increasing her understanding of the downloading of pictures to the computer. Secondly she planned to use the digital pictures taken to support her storytelling from real life scenarios.

In the course of this project it became evident that there was a tendency to focus on the functional uses of ICT in both home and school contexts without extending these into an analysis of their broader impact and a critique of their application for learning and meaning making. As a result, we devised a framework for learning that we called the C/ICT, which was a play on words because essentially the teachers wanted to "see" what the children were doing with ICT as well as consider the broader social and cognitive impact of these experiences and processes. In this way, the new media became more than tools or resources; rather, they were artifacts that had the potential to broaden experiences as well as extend the boundaries of exploration and influence knowledge-building processes.

The concept of the C/ICT (Figure 4.1) was informed by research carried out from a range of theoretical frameworks, including semiotics, critical sociology, and the multiliteracies approach, as well as developmental psychology. The pedagogic explication for the framework was based in the work of Durrant and Green (2000), who suggested that teachers can use a 3-D model to conceptualize the ways in which literacy is embodied in a curriculum. Durrant and Green's 3-D model contained three integrated dimensions: operational, cultural, and critical. The *operational* dimension involves technical competence and how-to knowledge. In ICT this involved knowledge about how to turn the device on and make it work, opening up files and documents and using Web pages (such as the Sesame Street Web page). The *cultural* dimension involves understanding how texts and technologies operate in the world and how they are used by individuals and groups, either in school or outside it. The focus is on both making meaning from texts and creating texts that make meaning for others. The *critical* dimension involves understanding that there is no one universal truth, and in any story or any curriculum what is told and studied is selective. The critical dimension is important in evaluating the impact of new technologies in our lives and the lives of others and involves a consideration of issues around social justice and equity.

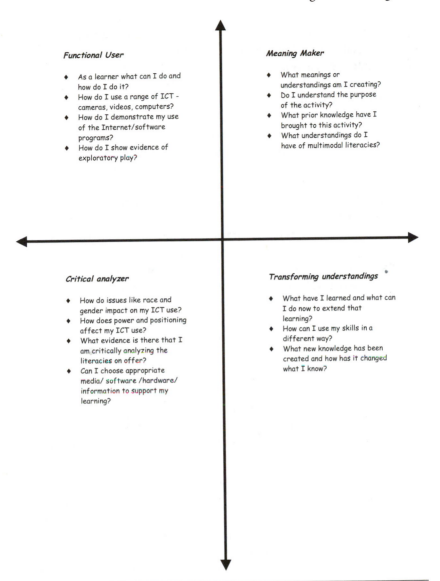

Functional User

♦ As a learner what can I do and how do I do it?
♦ How do I use a range of ICT - cameras, videos, computers?
♦ How do I demonstrate my use of the Internet/software programs?
♦ How do I show evidence of exploratory play?

Meaning Maker

♦ What meanings or understandings am I creating?
♦ Do I understand the purpose of the activity?
♦ What prior knowledge have I brought to this activity?
♦ What understandings do I have of multimodal literacies?

Critical analyzer

♦ How do issues like race and gender impact on my ICT use?
♦ How does power and positioning affect my ICT use?
♦ What evidence is there that I am critically analyzing the literacies on offer?
♦ Can I choose appropriate media/ software /hardware/ information to support my learning?

Transforming understandings

♦ What have I learned and what can I do now to extend that learning?
♦ How can I use my skills in a different way?
♦ What new knowledge has been created and how has it changed what I know?

Figure 4.1 The C/ICT framework

The aim was not for the C/ICT to become a checklist to be ticked off, and so it was constructed in such a manner that the teachers could explore their pedagogies and draw on personal learning stories (Podmore and Carr 1999) to create learning scenarios that could be contextualized within the frame of the C/ICT. It was also hoped that this process would inform subsequent planning and be more conducive for learning.

Monica used the C/ICT framework to consider the range of ICT-related activities that Julie engaged in with the digital camera at home. She indicated in her reflective journal that the visit had enabled her to link experiences that she planned in the school context more effectively after realizing that Julie had access to and could use a range of ICTs. For example, she realized that it would be useful for Julie to take digital photos of a sequence of events, such as eating her lunch which started with opening the box, went on to eating the food, then throwing away the rubbish, and finally going to play with friends. Then she could create a narrative based on the sequence to show her use of language as well as her understanding about time. Moreover, she indicated that the C/ICT framework made her think beyond the functional uses of ICT. She was aware that there was much more to consider and that she needed to plan to incorporate the meaning-making, critical, and transformative aspects of using new technologies with her children. Accordingly, she summarized her observations of Julie in the following way, which was a much broader view than she had previously considered:

Functional

- Uses or has experiences with a range of ICTs—video, TV, digital camera, video camera, computer, radio cassette player, interactive toys, and kitchen appliances.
- J is able to operate and use the various ICTs appropriately and engages in play most obviously on the computer. She is not afraid to have a go and keeps clicking to see what will happen when exploring.

Meaning maker

- Adds to her understanding of the Paint program after the visit by the older girls., e.g., she is able to now use fill and draw pictures with lines/color function.
- Realizes that the activities on the computer are fun.
- Is developing an understanding of how multimodal literacies work, e.g., CD-ROM icon changing to picture icon, process for accessing the games.

Critical analyzer

- J aware of uses for camera and how they can record family events.
- The older girls gave J more information about the Paint program, which she was able to use.
- Able to indicate differences between the two digital cameras and what they are used for.

Transforming understandings

- Was able to tell the difference between drawing with pencil and drawing with the computer—"You can change the color of the line on the computer but you can't do that with a pencil."
- J was able to talk about her understandings of pattern that she had learned from playing Solitaire on the computer.

COMPUTER GAMES

One thing that became evident in the techno tour was that all of the children had computer and/or video games. Most of the games were specifically dedicated to video game consoles, but the families also had a number of games on CD-ROM. First, there were the educational games. The games were usually related to drilling the "basic skills," that is spelling, phonics, and mathematical operations (i.e., adding, subtracting, multiplying, and dividing). Additionally, many families had CD-ROM-based computer games. These games were less sophisticated in terms of quality, scope, and visuals than the video games that came with consoles such as PlayStation, Nintendo, and Sega, but nevertheless they constituted a major form of activity for the children in the homes that were visited.

The literature reveals that computer games constitute an important part of young children's lives out of school (e.g., Provenzo 1992). Consequently, a number of out-of-school programs and vacation programs with a particular focus on games, either playing or designing them, have arisen to provide places where children from disadvantaged areas can play games of varying types in an informal learning environment (Cole 1996; Edwards 2002).

After-school programs are becoming increasingly popular as places where children go when the school day has ended and parents are still at work and not able to supervise their offspring. These contexts have demonstrated that game and design environments are conducive to the development of effective teaching and learning scenarios in which children are actively engaged with materials and ideas that promote collaborative and individual learning. Two programs that are exemplars of the practice are Computer Clubhouse and the Fifth Dimension.

Resnick and his colleagues at the Massachusetts Institute of Technology (MIT) Media Lab created Computer Clubhouse so that children who might not otherwise have the opportunity to become digitally fluent can do so more easily. He defined digital fluency as not only being able to use digital technologies but also being able to "construct things of significance" with them (Resnick 2001, 49). Computer Clubhouses are contexts in which young people could design and create things such as art, animations, simulations, multimedia presentations, musical compositions, Web sites, and robotic constructions using new media.

The first Computer Clubhouse was set up in South Boston in 1993, but now the concept has been incorporated into centers all over the world. They are different from the usual community-based programs in that the aim is not to teach basic skills of computing or provide opportunities to play games but rather to "help young people learn to express themselves and gain confidence as learners" (Resnick 2001, 51). To achieve these goals, the participants create projects that are viable, make use of available materials and artifacts, deploy effective strategies and find alternatives if they are not successful, collaborate in teams, and view a project from multiple perspectives. Basically, this amounts to how to initiate and manage a project from start to successful completion. In this way the Computer Clubhouse is both structured and flexible, and learners are supported to achieve their goals.

The data from the project illustrate the ways in which participation has transformed the lives of students who have not experienced success in traditional schooling. One of the participants stated:

> At the Clubhouse, I was free to do what I wanted, learn what I wanted. Whatever I did was just for me. If I had taken computer courses [in school], there would have been all those assignments. Here I could be totally creative. (Quoted in Resnick 2001, 55)

Resnick, like others, realizes that the wealthiest and most productive nations are those in which the education system reflects the needs of the citizens who inhabit them. He maintains that "new technology is changing not only what students *should* learn, but also what they *can* learn" (2001, 60). This means that concepts and ideas that might have been inaccessible can now be experienced and understood in the context of new learning with ICT. Correspondingly, he thinks that new curricula should not be put into boxes or disciplines for children who are organized in hierarchical age groups. There should be less emphasis on knowing "stuff" and more on how to investigate phenomena so that we are able to build and extend our knowledge about our world to make it a better place for all citizens and other living things. This will mean, as Resnick and others suggest, utilizing project-based approaches that engage students for extended periods of time so that they learn how to learn, and in so doing can make a valuable contribution to society. These ideas resonate with the notion of knowledge-building communities, which can be based in schools and communities at the local level and can also extend to global contexts.

The Fifth Dimension centers are grounded in cultural-historical activity theory (Cole 1996) and provide contexts in which children can learn via play and specifically can engage in computer and other technologically based learning opportunities. The centers are linked to universities, so a community of children, university students, and academics as well as adult community members is included. In this way the Fifth Dimension becomes a "powerful socially oriented educational activity" (Cole 1996, 298).

Structurally the environment is a maze constructed around numerous rooms that contain computer games to be mastered. There are a range of games in the rooms, and each has task cards associated with it. It is embedded in the rules of the Fifth Dimension that a learner has to complete a specific level of achievement before moving on to the next room or game. There are three levels of proficiency: beginning, good, and excellent. The activities include not only playing the game but also writing letters or notes to others, writing in a personal journal, contributing to a hints book, making videos, and creating artworks representing the knowledge gained and also the strategies deployed during the learning process. The Fifth Dimension has a mystical side. It is ruled by a wizard, who gave it to children as a gift, a place where they could learn and play, and it was constructed by the Entity, who is available via e-mail for questioning. Thus the Fifth Dimension is an activity system in which children can choose to participate in various technological and communicative activities at a level that they feel comfortable with. Undergraduate university students act as the wizard's assistants in this system to support the children in their learning and are able to extend the children's thinking and actions within the context of the zone of proximal development (ZPD). The Fifth Dimension can also be regarded as a cultural context for new learning, since "enculturation into this system involves simultaneously the acquisition of knowledge, changing role structures, and new ways of mediating one's interactions through the artefacts the culture makes available" (Cole 1996, 305).

Studies have shown that children who participate in the Fifth Dimension perform at a higher level in specialized tasks than those who have not (Blanton et al. 2000; Nicolopoulou and Cole 1993). Children who have participated also perform better in the more formal statewide measures of reading and mathematics. This is important since the majority of Fifth Dimension sites have been established in disadvantaged areas, and one of the program's initial goals was related to redressing the imbalance of access that has been characterized as the "digital divide." If such programs can provide opportunities for children who do not have computers at home, or indeed in their schools, they provide a vital social and educational function in giving opportunities to these students who would not otherwise have the opportunities to use new technologies.

Such out-of-school contexts have demonstrated the ways in which children can learn skills that are necessary for the twenty-first century in informal contexts that have engagement and learning as their stated goals within the context of the use of tools such as computers. As previously noted, much of what occurs in school today was designed around old learning and preparing for the industrial age; hence the focus on knowing facts and repeating routine procedures. However, these skills are becoming used less and less, and skills associated with being collaborative, creative, flexible, and knowing strategies for effective problem posing and solving are regarded as more important. After-school and community programs are leading the way in illustrating the creative solutions to problems that exist in school systems and should impact on decision making in schools themselves.

It has been noted that computer-based mathematical activity can be a powerful learning context for children (e.g., Battista and Clements 1986; Clements 1987; Yelland 1999, 2002a), and the use of computer games to study conceptual and skill development in mathematics is increasingly important. However, while there is some information about specific environments that may promote the use and development of mathematical thinking, not a great deal of work has been done with reference to integrating existing commercial software into mathematics programs or developing specific software as part of the creation and design of curricula for the new century. This is an important area for research since, for example, it has been demonstrated that students' use of video and computer games in out-of-school contexts affects their interactions with the media in school in pervasive ways (Upitis 1998). Upitis has shown, for example, that students in her study judge computer games in the school context against the video games that they play at home. In the E GEMS project the researchers found significant differences in performance based on gender (Inkpen et al. 1994) and that the role of the teacher is critical in explicating the mathematical inferences in games. They stated, "Without specific guidance from a teacher or mentor, it would appear that many students, and significantly more girls than boys . . . will not detect the underlying mathematical concepts that might be embedded within a computer game" (De Jean et al. 1999, 216). Other research has also highlighted the importance of the teacher in making mathematical connections explicit to learners (Leitze 1997).

It is apparent that computer games have the potential to engage children in learning in ways that were not possible without them. Game contexts motivate children to play with ideas, interact, and collaborate with peers in sharing strategies and articulating ideas, and in doing so they acquire skills for learning and new knowledge that seem to be adaptable to new and different contexts. The ways in which they do this is still not clearly understood.

In an attempt to explore this further a study was designed to examine and describe the ways in which children chose, used, and evaluated computer software created to develop particular mathematical processes and thinking.[1] It sought to add to knowledge by identifying the levels of interest, mathematical understanding, and learning of students as they engaged with computer games in an after-school context. It was particularly concerned with obtaining data that would shed light on several areas:

- *Mathematical learning,* via descriptions of the mathematical understandings that emerged as children played and interacted in computer-based contexts, and the ways in which children developed and refined their mathematical strategies and representations as they gained experience with the various examples of software.
- *Social processes,* by examining the ways in which the design and content of the software influenced social interactions while it was being played, and if these affected how the children viewed the software. Of particular interest here were constructions of gender, which may be influential since computer games have been noted as being more appealing to boys than to girls (e.g., Cassell and Jenkins 1998).
- *Which features of computer software appealed to children,* in particular those that initially attracted children to a game and those with a sustaining effect. Additionally, it was thought to be important to consider how teachers and children selected software for use and the ways in which they made sense of the various characteristics of the different games.

Twenty children ranging from five to twelve years of age participated in the study, which was located in a suburban after-school care program. The children played the games on two laptop computers that were adjacent to other activities in the hall where the program was located. The children were interviewed before the study commenced about their experience with computers and computer activities in home and school contexts, and when the study was completed they were interviewed for a second time to ascertain their favorite programs, what they particularly liked about them, and what they most liked about playing the games in the after-school context.

The children had access to a range of twenty-five games that were all mathematical in content, and initially there were no restrictions placed on their use (after a few weeks we had to introduce time restrictions, as the children claimed that some were "hogging" the computer time). It was immediately evident that three games were the most popular, as evidenced by their almost continuous use: The Logical Journey of the Zoombinis, Counting on Frank, and Carmen Sandiego Math Detective.

Some of the young children found it difficult to articulate the reasons they liked the games and mainly gave answers like: "Don't know" or "It was fun," while the older children were able to focus on specific aspects of the game that they enjoyed. For example, Divy, a seventh grader, said: "Zoombinis—because you can go through the levels and sometimes like showed some things—the levels were good. It's fun to play and you can choose your Zoombinis—make them how you want." Thus, for Divy the different levels enabled him to set goals so that he could progress up through them. Additionally, he seemed to enjoy the fact that he had been able to create his own Zoombinis using the four attributes and in his playing of the game was very careful to ensure their safety. Similarly, Kyle (also in seventh grade) said: "Zoombinis, because I like adventure games more than other types and like inventing Zoombinis." Hannah (third grade) said: "Zoombinis and Madeline. I just like them. Good pictures and interesting things to do."

Overall, there seemed to be three features of games that made them popular with this group of children. These were:

- *Puzzle format.* These games were more attractive than those with simple activities that were an end in themselves or resulted in a reward or trinket for effort expended. Maddy (grade one) said she liked Secret Paths "because you find stones . . . I like the girls and like what they made out of the computer. . . . I liked when they told us about their mums and friends said and the pictures. . . . I liked the pathways pictures."

- *A design element combined with a narrative.* The children in this study enjoyed making their own characters (e.g., Zoombinis) and chose as their three favorite games ones that were set in a story context. For example, Kyle stated: "My favorite is Zoombinis . . . because I like adventure games more than other types and I like inventing Zoombinis." The children in fact became very possessive about their Zoombinis and made comments like "Don't you dare hurt my Zoombinis" (from Richard, a fourth grader, when the troll in one of the puzzles "threatened" his creations). Players also engaged in conversation with the characters as they were playing. Richard, for example, commented, "Okay, we push on. Come on, you guys you have to come with us. . . . I saved your lives, guys, so you should be thanking me. I did quite a lot of work for you."

- *Software that catered to a variety of levels of interest and ability.* This was evident in Zoombinis, which Marcus indicated was his favorite because "you can go on different levels," but also in games such as Math Workshop, which had three different levels; Divy (seventh grade) said he "could change the levels and watch the gorilla knock the pins down."

Mathematical Understandings

The data revealed that for the younger children, that is, those up to fourth grade, mathematics was mainly related to numbers and sums. The older children, especially those in sixth and seventh grades, recognized that Zoombinis was mathematics because it had "puzzles" and "combinations." In fact, one of the things that appealed to children in this age group about games such as Zoombinis was that the mathematics was "cool maths—really hard maths" (Kyle, seventh grade). In contrast, Kyle noted that Math Workshop was math too but "it was really easy—boring maths." Kyle also thought that he had learned "new maths stuff" by playing Zoombinis, because of the different levels. The younger children did not seem to recognize the shape activities (e.g., in James Discovers Math) as mathematics. Maddy (first grade) said she liked the shapes game in James Discovers Math and when asked if it was math she said, "No—it's matching pictures."

Of interest here were not only the differences across the age range but also the fact that the older children seemed to enjoy being challenged in the games, whereas the younger group just wanted to play the games in easy mode for fun. One exception was Zoombinis, which was always challenging to all the children who played it—and *all* the children played it. One afternoon in the third week Maddy (first grade) was offering advice to Kevin (fifth grade) about how to get the Zoombinis across the bridge in the first activity based on finding their similar attributes. It was Kevin's first time with the program, and Maddy had already had experience and success with this particular game and could advise him. This would not have been possible in school contexts and provided Maddy with the opportunity to feel good about the fact that she could make a contribution to the successful experience of an older student.

Interactions During Game Playing

The nature and extent of the interactions while the children were play-ing the computer games were interesting and complex. Among the fac-tors that influenced the ways in which the children interacted were:

- The environment—free choice and after-school context
- The software design—puzzle and narrative context versus activity-based separate activities
- The age and gender of the children

The after-school environment was very conducive to interactions and collaborations. As previously stated, there were no restrictions placed on the children in terms of what they could play unless someone else was using it. The physical space helped in this as well—the laptop computers were placed on large tables and children could sit beside each other and bring chairs over to perch on. This still meant that one, perhaps two chil-dren had the main roles, but the space allowed for up to six other chil-dren to be involved in the experience. This is a stark contrast to school use of the games, where a maximum of two is usually the norm.

This context was also more conducive for playing the games for extended periods of time. The children reported that when they played games in class time they often were told to stop right in the middle of an exciting part and rarely finished a defined section of a game. This form of organization favors short games without a narrative, and many of the drill and practice games are organized so that they can be played for short periods of time. However, with software such as Zoombinis, Counting on Frank, and Carmen Sandiego it is useful to have longer periods of time for playing, since in the short term gains are small. Additionally, the activity-based software packages are more easily accommodated in math curricula, since they focus on traditional concept areas such as number, measurement, and space, whereas games such as Zoombinis focus more on problem-solving and reasoning skills.

Further, games such as Zoombinis, Counting on Frank, and Carmen Sandiego all afforded opportunities to share strategies and collaborate, since they contained problem-solving activities. Simple activities such as adding 3 and 6 or multiplying 6 and 7 do not tend to result in collab-orative behaviors. In this way, software programs that were "not simple maths" (in the words of third grader Matthias) were characterized by much higher levels of interactions than those that had a number of short and simple games.

It was also apparent that some programs were liked by both boys and girls—Zoombinis, Counting on Frank, and Carmen San Diego fell into

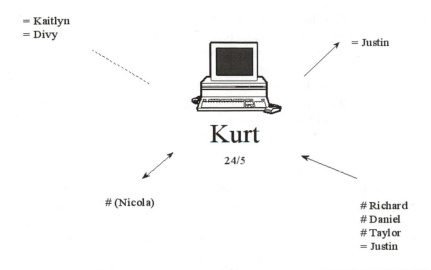

Figure 4.2 Interactions with Kurt in after-school computer club

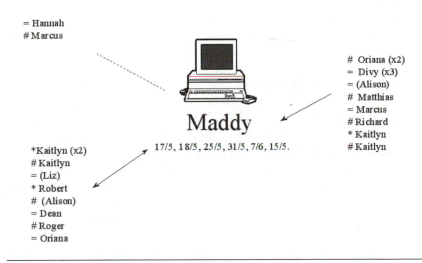

Figure 4.3 Interactions with Maddy in after-school computer club

this category—but that other games were favored by one gender. For example, Madeline was preferred by girls only, while boys, especially the younger ones (five and six years old), really enjoyed Land Before Time, which features dinosaurs.

The nature and extent of interactions was mapped for each child and showed considerable variation. We characterized some children as watchers (rather than doers). They would offer advice to their peers on some occasions but infrequently played a game by themselves. They would also stand by while a large team of players persisted to the end of a complex problem-solving game. The variety and style of interactions are presented as diagrammatic representations in Figures 4.2 and 4.3.

Figure 4.2 maps the interactions with a fourth grader, Kurt, on May 24. It reveals that when Kurt was playing Zoombinis on this day over a period of 48 minutes, three peers, Richard (fourth grade), Daniel (fifth grade), and Taylor (third grade), spent more than 2 minutes interacting with him by asking and responding to questions and making general comments about the game. Justin (seventh grade) came to join the group for less than 2 minutes when Kurt asked him a question about strategy, and Kaitlyn (first grade) and Divy (seventh grade) stood and watched for a short time (less than 2 minutes). Additionally, the researcher (Nicola) engaged Kurt in conversation about what he and his peers were doing while they were playing the game and Kurt was at the keyboard. These data are a stark contrast to those for games such as JumpStart or Math Workshop, where there was minimal or no interaction between the children.

Figure 4.3 shows all the people that Maddy interacted with over a period of six sessions. The interactions were both two-way, as shown by the double-headed arrow, and also one way, with peers offering Maddy advice to which she responded in some way, as shown by the arrow pointing in. This means that while Maddy was on the computer playing games she both asked for advice and interacted with respondents. She also listened to advice from others without verbally reacting. The range of peers that Maddy interacted with spanned all age levels. There were only two children (Hannah and Marcus) who watched Maddy without offering comments or asking questions. The timing of the interactions is indicated: whole sessions are indicated by an asterisk (*), more than two minutes but not the whole sessions is indicated by a pound sign (#), and less than two minutes is shown by an equals sign (=).

It was evident that the interactions were very unpredictable; still, the nature of the after-school program was such that rarely was there no interaction at all. This was in direct contrast to data being collected at the same time with the same games in a classroom-based study where interactions were generally limited or controlled by the teacher.

The results indicated that well-designed computer games act as a stimulus for learning and engagement with mathematical ideas and processes and afford the opportunity for children to participate in collaborative problem solving in new and dynamic ways. Observing children in an after-school context highlighted differences between in-school and out-of-school learning opportunities, which may inform teachers and caregivers in both settings. Overall, it would seem that the after-school environment provided a valuable context for exploring mathematical concepts with technology. One of the most pleasing aspects was the interaction of children across age groups, which is not usually possible within school settings. The data reveal that such interactions were of mutual benefit to all age groups in terms of improving self-esteem, confidence, and success with the game content.

VIDEO GAMES

After-school contexts may provide a range of games that are basically educational in their focus, but in their own homes and those of others, children have access to various video games that may not conform to expectations of the education system, since they are often regarded as violent or could not be justified in terms of their appropriateness and alignment with educational objectives.

The worldwide interactive entertainment business market is expected to grow from approximately $28.5 billion in 2005 to around $42 billion in 2010 (DFC Intelligence 2005). Total U.S. retail sales of video game hardware, software, and peripherals was $10.3 billion in 2002 and is increasing steadily (RocSearch 2005). One only has to watch the TV news and read the newspapers to see the impact that the launch of a new console has when thousands of eager people crowd stores to purchase the latest system (Yi 2004).

Gee commented, "When people learn to play video games, they are learning a new *literacy*" (2003, 13). He extended this notion by saying that literacy in this sense is a broad conceptualization that goes beyond the traditional view of literacy as the ability to read and write. Gee maintained that we need to regard representations such as images, symbols, graphs, diagrams, and artifacts as well as other visual forms as being as important as language for communication, and that people who are not able to interpret these visual representations effectively are seriously disadvantaged in contemporary times. He extended the consideration of multimodality to semiotic domains, which he regarded as being constituted by more than one modality (e.g., written language, images, equations, symbols, sounds, gestures) to communicate specific types of meanings. He considers video games as a semiotic domain, and suggests that in the twenty-first century it is not enough to be simply "print literate"; rather, people need to be fluent in a number of semiotic domains to be regarded as literate and to function effectively.

Table 4.1 Learning and Video Games

The learner realizes . . .	
About self (identity)	That s/he can use active exploration to construct new ideas
	That s/he has the ability to recognize and apply context-specific use of signs
	That s/he can take risks in explorations
	That s/he wants to actively learn to engage and take on role of investigator/explorer; s/he realizes the connections/disconnections of each form of identity
	That s/he is a learner
	The potential for achieving successful outcomes (e.g., mastery)
	That responses to feedback require refinement or change in approach; is able to deploy appropriate strategies using relevant tools
	That s/he can apply knowledge to the situation and build an increasingly sophisticated knowledge base from action and interaction in communities of practice
About the task	That the task is achievable, and so the learner can determine an effective starting place as an introduction to the semiotic domain; can then continue knowing that the task and solutions will become progressively more complex and challenging
	What the task/activity structure is, and sees that mastery is followed by consolidation via practice and small units of skill/knowledge built up from basic to complex
	That instructions need to be clear and specific
	That the activity is structured to promote active exploration, inquiry and problem solving and enables different routes to solution.
	That the skills/knowledge acquired can be adapted to new or subsequent activities/tasks
About the context	That there are links/connections between tasks and strategies that may be effective
	That s/he can analyze actions/task requirements in relation to existing experiences and can interpret the relevance of strategies to be used
	That s/he can facilitate movement between multimodal texts and encourages modification of strategies to reach goals; possesses understandings about different representations and how they can be probed/explored
	That there are advantages to practicing strategies so that generalizations and connections can be created
	That s/he needs to monitor what has to be done and its relevance for use again in a novel context
	That the use of appropriate artifacts is required for successful solution; shares strategies with others

About the culture	That learning occurs in a cultural context that impacts on decision making (consciously) so that choices can be made about paths/solutions/strategies to use/follow; critical reflection on choices should be made in the context of their relationship to cultural viewpoints of varying perspectives That s/he is an individual in a particular context and simultaneously a member of a community that can support and extend individual and social learning opportunities

Source: Adapted from Gee 2003.

> To understand or produce any word, symbol, image, or artifact in a given semiotic domain, a person must be able to situate the meaning of that word, symbol, image or artifact within embodied experiences of action, interaction, or dialogue in or about the domain. (Gee 2003, 24)

Gee asserted that video games are powerful learning environments, because playing in the video game domain can act as a precursor for mastering other semiotic domains related to new technologies. He noted thirty-six learning principles that account for why video games are effective as learning contexts; an adapted version of the ideas is presented in Table 4.1.

The table illustrates that when successfully playing video games, the learner comes to important realizations about the self as a learner, features of the task, aspects of context, and the cultural conditions in which the game playing is taking place. These items are neither hierarchical or sequential. They might occur simultaneously at a particular point in time but will not all occur to the same degree (and may even not occur at all) within the context of one game.

Video games allow players to actively construct ideas via a process of exploration that requires them to take risks and associates these with consequences. One of the major features of these games is that players report they wholeheartedly take on a character in the course of playing the game but can just as easily return to their daily lives when not playing the game. As previously stated, Vygotsky (1978) conceptualized the notion of the zone of proximal development (ZPD) to denote the area between what a person can achieve independently and what the person can do when scaffolded by an adult or more knowledgeable peer. In video game playing, learners are overtly aware of this and seek support from the game itself as well as other game players and online support systems, which provide valuable information and strategies that can lead to important breakthroughs in explorations. The enthusiasm and persistence of game players is often mystifying to adults who do not share their passion. Yet is it evident that these are confident learners who want to achieve success and mastery, and they have been able to build an increasingly sophisticated knowledge base from actions and interactions in their various communities of game-playing practices.

The content, structure, and narratives of games vary considerably, but there are general characteristics that seem to signal or even guarantee the success of any particular game. Yet it is very hard to predict success or failure in this arena when new games appear on the market. Video game players seem to have incredible persistence and thrive on the challenge of the game (Gee 2003; Prensky 2001), but it is essential that they realize the game can be mastered. They also need clear and specific directions and a game structure that becomes progressively more challenging as they move through it. This structure then involves mastery, via experimentation with opportunities for consolidation via practice. Then, once this is achieved the structure ensures that they are directed to more complex activities and the cycle repeats. None of this will occur unless the player is actively building up knowledge and skills in context. A side benefit is that some of these skills are generalizable and can be utilized in new games if deep learning has taken place.

In this way, the context of game playing is important, and the learner needs to make connections between the game's tasks or requirements and adapt them to new games as part of the learner's repertoire of skills deployment. This linking to previous experiences, or tapping into the existing knowledge base, is an important precondition of learning. We don't learn in a vacuum and have to contextualize what we are doing. This is the essence of situation cognition (Brown, Collins, and Duguid 1989), which has been shown to be a powerful condition for learning. Other relevant features of context involve facilitating movement between multimodal texts and the appropriateness of various representations in each so that meaning can be made, practiced, and reutilized in a variety of instances.

An important aspect of context is the culture of video games. Beyond self-realization is an understanding of context and culture, which implies knowledge about the nature of the games and the understanding that they are played in communities of practice in which members generally support each other in a quest for mastery. This enables players to develop a critical capacity about information and strategies, using them to achieve maximum benefit. The persistence and dedication of video game players in this regard has to be marveled at by teachers, who must try to tap into this as they convey to their students information the teachers consider fundamental to their productive lives in out-of-school contexts, both now and in the future.

Buckingham and Scanlon (2003) have noted the features of games that seem to make them most attractive to players. They suggested that games are complex multimodal environments that stimulate the eye with stunning visual imagery. The games offer contexts in which players are able to choose the directions they can take within a controlling structure of rules (though often the rules can be negotiated, depending upon the circumstances). Games are usually structured so that they incorporate a significant challenge, which can only be mastered over time with a large number of hours of engagement. This involves the player-learner in utilizing a gamut of cognitive activities, including collecting and synthesizing new knowledge as the game proceeds, extending memory capacity, solving and posing problems, collecting and using artifacts, strategic planning, and testing hypotheses. Buckingham and Scanlon contended that these features not only make game playing attractive as a play pastime but also impact on the intellectual, emotional, and physiological being of the individual within this new social milieu. It is important to note that neither educational software nor the school experience seems to have embraced these features.

Games have become an integral part of the lives of children and thus rate highly in peer group culture, where they are frequently the focus of activities. This is especially true for boys, but increasingly girls are becoming more fascinated by and absorbed in online Internet games. Gee (2003) has suggested that, rather than bemoan the number of hours students spend playing such games, we should make a closer examination of the features that attract players and learn from them in our design of the educational experience. These features parallel what we know works in schools but don't always practice because other imperatives, such as the current emphasis on testing, are the focus of much classroom activity.

SUMMARY

This chapter has explored children's learning in informal out-of-school contexts and suggested that knowledge about these environments and the use of new technologies in them can provide useful information to teachers about the experiences that children bring into their classrooms. Information about the child from such contexts enriches the schooling experience, since teachers are able to plan for learning more effectively when they recognize the richness of the total experiences that a child has. Data from a range of sources has been provided to illustrate children's engagement with ICT and how these technologies might be used in a variety of ways to record events, for recreation, and for learning.

These after-school contexts do not have curricula and the children are not distinguished by age and ability in any way. Some have a particular structure (e.g., the maze of the Fifth Dimension), and others (e.g., Computer Clubhouse) have rules that prohibit the playing of games but rather focus on the creation and design of new games. Nevertheless, they provide information about engagement and voluntary participation that is sustained and enthusiastic and would be desirable for the education experience in schools. In Chapter 5 the focus shifts to learning in schools and the ways in which we can extend the engagement and passion so vividly illustrated in these out-of-school contexts.

NOTE

1. ARC Discovery. Yelland. "Through the Glass Wall: Computer Games for Mathematical Empowerment," 1999–2001.

5

NEW WAYS OF LEARNING IN SCHOOL

You're in control. Is there anywhere you wanna go? You're in control. Is there anything you wanna know? The future's for discovering . . .

—*Coldplay, "Square One"*

NEW TIMES, NEW LEARNING

So far in the book I have described new times and new learning along with the associated rethinking of curriculum and pedagogy that needs to accompany it for effective knowledge building. In this chapter I will provide examples of what this means for reconceptualizing the new basics and laying the foundations to become numerate and multiliterate in the information age. This will be supported with work samples derived from empirical research studies with teachers. In all of the research projects, the teachers have been active researchers of their own contexts and have been involved in a process of professional learning that has required them not only to make a dramatic shift in their thinking but also to do this in the context of existing curriculum constraints, while others have had a new paradigm installed from above and were required to adapt as a policy imperative. The focus of the work has primarily been in relation to numeracy, but it became evident over the course of the project that compartmentalizing numeracy and literacy, and indeed viewing curricula as separate boxes or domains of knowledge called subjects or disciplines, was not helpful when discussing effective learning contexts for the twenty-first century.

BECOMING NUMERATE WITH ICT

Numeracy and the importance of developing a numerate populace who can function effectively with the practical mathematical demands of everyday life in the twenty-first century are major concerns of many organizations worldwide (e.g., Australian Council for Educational Research 1990; Department of Education, Training, and Youth Affairs 2000; Her Majesty's Inspectorate 1998; Ministerial Council on Education, Employment, Training, and Youth Affairs 1999; NCTM 1998).

The process of becoming numerate is continuous, and the years from birth to eight represent an age of unparalleled growth when the foundations of skills and concepts are established (Anning and Edwards 1999; NCTM 2000). These years also represent a time for children to establish positive attitudes toward mathematics and the ways in which it can contribute to everyday life. Children use a variety of mathematical ideas and processes in informal ways in the years before they attend school (Baroody and Wilkins 1999; Greenes 1999; Hunting 1999). They develop understandings about money when shopping and about time as they embark on journeys in the family car or on trains. Such informal learning contexts are enriched when parents or caregivers support the learning via reading stories, highlighting real-world applications involving numeracy concepts, and making links between numeracy and play activities. This learning should be extended in schools, and the first step would seem to be having a shared understanding about what numeracy is and how we can create contexts for becoming numerate that incorporate the effective use of new technologies.

The National Numeracy Project, convened in the United Kingdom in 1996, included this conceptualization of numeracy:

> Numeracy means knowing about numbers and number operations. More than this, it includes an ability and inclination to apply numerical understanding and skills to solve problems, including those involving money and measures. It also includes familiarity with the ways in which numerical information is gathered by counting and measuring, and is presented in graphs, charts and tables (quoted in Straker 2000, 41).

Historically in the United Kingdom, the discipline of mathematics that came to be enacted in schools was primarily based on number and operating with numbers, with subsidiary importance being placed on measurement (incorporating the use of number) and geometry for the purpose of being able to use the skills and knowledge of the discipline for problem solving. This was despite attempts to broaden school curricula beyond the subject areas to a more general thematic approach that crossed disciplines and was more closely aligned with investigations of real phenomena and themes of study.

In the United States the term *numeracy* is not commonly used; instead the National Council of the Teachers of Mathematics (NCTM) has incorporated the notion of "mathematical literacy" or "quantitative literacy" into its reform agenda. Devlin suggested that it was essential to differentiate between mathematics and quantitative literacy and noted that the latter

> comprises a reasonable sense of number, including the ability to estimate orders of magnitude within a certain range, an ability to understand numerical data the ability to read a chart or graph, and the ability to follow an argument based on numerical or statistical evidence. (2000, 24)

Devlin saw the responsibility for quantitative literacy, like that of literacy, as being the basic responsibility of *all* teachers and contended that the goal of mathematics in schools should be related to developing an awareness of and an appreciation for its nature, extent, and relevance to modern life. In this way, mathematics in schools would be broad and provide students with the skills and knowledge base necessary for effective functioning in their lives; it would also include "imaginative use of all available media" (Devlin 2000, 25).

In Australia the Commonwealth government published *Numeracy, a Priority for All*, which recognized that "being numerate enables adults to function effectively in their everyday lives" (Department of Education, Training, and Youth Affairs 2000, 2). The report noted that in Australia numeracy was viewed in a broad way that went beyond knowing about numbers and the ways in which they are used in different contexts. It refers to a 1997 report from the Australian Association of Mathematics Teachers, which proposed:

> To be numerate is to use mathematics effectively to meet the general demands of life at home, in paid work, and for participation in community and civic life.
>
> In school education, numeracy is a fundamental component of learning, performance, discourse and critique across all areas of the curriculum. It involves the disposition to use, in context, a combination of:
> - Underpinning mathematical concepts and skills from across the discipline (numerical, spatial, graphical, statistical and algebraic);
> - Mathematical thinking and strategies;

- General thinking skills;
- Grounded appreciation of context. (Cited in Department of Education, Training, and Youth Affairs 2000, 3)

In an interesting study, Zevenbergen (2004) sought to investigate technologizing numeracy by exploring what different generations of people regarded as being effective in mathematics and numeracy in the twenty-first century. Older people viewed numeracy in terms of adeptness in using number to calculate and solve problems, while the younger group (twenty-two years and under) regarded statistics and measurement as being more important. Additionally, the role of technology in people's lives was a major distinguishing feature between the two cohorts. Senior people rated the capacity of effective mental calculations as being of major importance for everyday problem solving since they regarded many of the problems to be solved as originating when machines (calculators and computers) malfunctioned, when in fact this rarely occurred. In contrast, younger people saw technology as a tool that enabled them to work more effectively at higher or big-picture levels and released them from the most mundane aspects of performing calculations. These different conceptualizations of numeracy influenced the ways in which each group defined the role of mathematics and their expectations of what constituted technological competence in their various workplaces:

> Senior participants were more likely to describe issues of mental computation as foundational skills and attributes needed for working effectively, younger people were more likely to see these as low order tasks that should be undertaken by technology and that their role was to identify problems and solve them using technology to support that solution. (Zevenbergen 2004, 114)

Research on the impact of teachers' beliefs on curriculum reform is of relevance here:

> If the mathematics teachers' beliefs are not congruent with the beliefs underpinning an educational reform, then the aftermath of such a mismatch can affect the degree of success of the innovations as well as the teachers' morale and willingness to implement further innovation. (Handal and Herrington 2003, 60)

With this in mind I have worked with teachers to discover the ways in which ICT impacted on their curriculum planning in mathematics and the ways in which they perceived numeracy to be linked to mathematics teaching and learning.

As previously noted, a fundamental problem associated with the use of computers in schools is that their use has been mapped onto existing curricula that were created in a noncomputer age. Thus, it is difficult for teachers to create opportunities for new explorations and understandings with ICT since the content of curricula and the assessment outcomes often inhibit this. Research has shown that we have a great deal of information about the ways in which new technologies are able to transform learning but school curricula essentially remain the same as they were in the last century (Tinker 1999; Yelland 1999, 2002c). Further, Resnick (1998, 2001) has urged us to regard the use of computers like that of any other materials we might find in schools, such as paints or blocks, since they are all useful for active learning, inquiry, and problem solving. He suggested that computers afford the opportunity for new types of explorations as well as for possibilities of sharing the strategies and findings with a wider community. This perspective, of course, requires a radical rethinking of curriculum that encapsulates contemporary notions about creativity, imagination, and design that provide opportunities for children to explore and investigate in ways that were not possible without the new technologies. It means that they will be able to generate new knowledge as well as learn about existing knowledge bases. Such an approach has already been suggested since "studies overwhelmingly suggest that computer-based technology is only one element in what must be a coordinated approach to improving curriculum, pedagogy, assessment and teacher development, and other aspects of school structure" (Roschelle et al. 2000, 78).

Additionally, in rethinking the structure of new curricula there has been an increasing recognition that curriculum decision making needs to take note of children's out-of-school experiences and build upon them. This has caused academics such as Dede, for example, to call on educators to "reshape children's learning experiences in and out of school to prepare them for a future quite different from the immediate past. Meeting this challenge involves teaching new skills, not simply teaching old skills better" (2000, 178)

Thus, there has been a recognition that we need to consider new ways of *thinking* and *doing* education. Traditionally, curricula in schools prepared students for an era in which they had to perform mechanistic tasks and learn routines for application. Such methods have long been outmoded, but the back-to-basics movement has been powerful in lobbying for curricula based on specific content and industrial modes of learning. In this way, and with the current emphasis on testing for accountability and comparison of nations (e.g., U.S. Department of

Education 2001), what remains is a system created in a previous era with little relevance to the lives of the young people who exist in it, except for some pockets of innovation in which there have been attempts to reconceptualize education and curricula so that we are able to prepare citizens for the twenty-first century.

In the previous chapter I described an after-school project, which we called the Glass Wall project, which in its first year took place in an after-school computer club. The second year the study was located in classrooms of teachers who were interested in incorporating computer games into their mathematics program. The study was aimed at exploring the mathematics learning that occurred while playing the games, and it became apparent that the children loved playing them even though the level of mathematics content was frequently well below their ability. The competitive nature of the game together with receiving prizes (e.g., certificates or tokens that enabled players to move to a new level) was often a great motivator for pursuing the games.

However, the most popular game, The Logical Journey of the Zoombinis, defied the trend of the mainstream drill and practice software that is usually available. The range of mathematical processes in Zoombinis is varied and requires a great deal of logical thinking, problem solving, and spatial understanding. There is no number work in the traditional sense of having to complete algorithms, but an ability to operate on numbers can be a valuable aid in some of the games that form the whole of the adventure with the Zoombinis. The games were not easy; in fact, one of the most salient observations was that the children who played this game loved the challenge, despite the fact that initially they did not have a lot of success. But such was their desire to help the Zoombinis to locate to a new land that they persevered and with scaffolding became adept at realizing what was required to solve the problems. The mathematics in Zoombinis was very different from that found in traditional mathematics curriculum. The following vignette illustrates the rich types of interactions that occurred when the children were playing the games and the sophisticated range of strategies that they used in order to solve the problems they faced:

S: Now let's try this one. I think it's mushrooms and pepperoni, this one. [He has watched another pair.]

T: So that's the olives that you tried.

S: Ah . . . try mushroom and pepperoni.

T: Now that tells you he likes the olives but he wants something else on them—so you have to find something else that he likes.

S: I don't think that's anything.

T&B: It's cheese.

S: Cheese?

T: It's cheese.

S: He doesn't like cheese—let me try.

B: I'll give him cheese again.

S: No, no, no, don't give him cheese . . . maybe this one.

B: We tried that one.

S: Hey, mister . . . do you like this?

B: It's the same thing.

S: Oh, okay. [They try another one.]

B: Oh, he likes it . . . he does like it.

S: Hmmm, something else he wants . . .

B: Give him cheese again.

S: No, give him this one—maybe he likes this one . . . Like that? Do you? . . . Ouch. [A Zoombini has gotten knocked.]

B: He loves it—he chucked it over.

T: What do you think you have to do now?

B: Ah, make him another pizza?

S: What?

B: Ask for more ingredients?

T: Make it with all of those things on it, so the olives . . .

S: Okay, we don't have that one or the cheese.

T: Hang on—didn't he not like that?

S: Yeah, he didn't like that, but we tried all six.

B: Put that one on as well—put all of them on it and see if he likes it.

T: Hang on.

S: Is there only one that we don't have?

T: Hang on—just think, he likes, you can see he likes olives, pepperoni, and mushrooms, so what do you think will happen if you put all of those three together?

B: He'll eat it?

S: Now how do we put it all together, though?

It was readily apparent that children could work collaboratively and individually with enthusiasm when they were playing the computer games. The data illustrated a range of social and cognitive interactions in which the children were discussing mathematical concepts with a high level of understanding, participating in problem posing and problem solving, and sharing effective strategies while articulating the reasons they worked. Since the games provided a context for exploration there were many examples of collaborations that yielded spontaneous oral conversations that enabled these young children (five and six years old) to practice and use their mathematical skills and understandings.

R: Here, can I, can I play around on it?

K: This is cool.

R: [He clicks on a creature.] Ugh, chickpeas . . . he spit something out, some green stuff.

K: Er, yuck . . . Press on that, um, circle thing.

R: Circle thing?

K: Yeah.

R: This thing?

K: Yeah, what does that do?

R: Er . . . [The color machine comes up.]

K: Wow.

R: Let's click this.

K: Yeah.

Both: Ah! [It makes a colored sphere.]

R: That's magic.

K: Click yellow.

R: I'll click blue . . . oh, we're making balls.

K: That makes that color . . . you can mix the colors up.

T: Yes, it's to see what color you've got.

K: What about yellow? [The other child finds how to change the shapes.] That's a good one.

R: That's awesome.

K: That's cool.

The study concluded that good-quality software could be accommodated in mathematics curricula to extend what was already being done and add a new dimension to the learning. This use of software in a structured way was also a stimulus for investigations across curricula and supported collaborative learning, which led to interactive social action in pairs or small groups. It was limited only by the small range of titles that were considered to be appropriate, and did not fundamentally change what was occurring in the content of the mathematics curriculum.

In a study that was concerned with reconceptualizing numeracy beyond simply regarding it as applying the skills and knowledge derived from mathematics in everyday contexts, we wanted to examine the ways in which new technologies could be used for rethinking numeracy in the new social context of the information age.[1] A part of the project was to derive a model for numeracy teaching that was relevant to the goal of being able to function effectively in everyday life in the twenty-first century, so that the model could act as a resource for teachers to use in their planning of learning experiences to ensure that they had contemporary relevance to the lives of the children.

The study involved twenty-two teachers in two schools over a period of three years. The schools were in the outer suburbs of a large metropolitan city in an Australian state where compulsory schooling begins at age five in a preparatory class. In the first year of the study, five classes and their teachers were observed in teaching and learning activities across the curriculum. It was considered to be important to ascertain understandings about the ways in which mathematics was taught and how the concepts and skills inherent to it might be applied across the traditional subject areas. At the commencement of the study and at the beginning of each subsequent school year the teachers were interviewed individually about their views and perceptions around education, mathematics, numeracy, and the use of ICT. Case study children were selected in the first year of the study, and their mathematics learning was documented over a period of three years.

Discovering how teachers conceptualized numeracy was regarded as a useful starting point for the project since we wanted to generate a new model for numeracy that not only was relevant to contemporary society but also reflected teacher beliefs and what they desired to inculcate in the children that they were teaching. The information gleaned from the interviews complemented that from the literature, and the model was generated from the intersection of theory and practice.

TEACHING MATHEMATICS AND BECOMING NUMERATE

In order to think about the role of mathematics and numeracy in the school curriculum we wanted to obtain a big-picture view from the teachers about what they regarded as the function of schools in the first instance, since this would impact on what they enacted in the daily program. It was apparent that teachers regarded schools as places to develop skills that were both social and related to disciplines. They thought, for example, that children needed to build confidence and skills to cope with their later lives, which in turn would enable them to become good citizens. Some teachers also indicated that a caring attitude was an important aspect that provided the context in which such skills and knowledge would be nurtured. For example:

MeadowlandsT1[2]: There is always some knowledge and know-how involved. But the last thing you would want is to pursue the facts. What I would be hoping to do as well as pursuing those things would be to develop thinking skills . . . and approaching skills, how to go about doing things. I would want in all subjects [the development of] creative thinking, thinking outside of the circle, thinking for yourself. Establish an atmosphere where children [at school] . . . and in later life have a have-a-go attitude. School as a place where children have a fair go and learn how to be out in the real world while they are still in school.

MeadowlandsT2: Social skills—want them to be able to work cooperatively in a group situation. Academic side of things—to be literate and numerate. Have a good general knowledge. Exposure to situations that they may not get at home (e.g., excursions etc.).

MeadowlandsT6: To teach kids, but also to teach them to learn for themselves . . . to be their own learners and to take risks and to prepare them for their future. So . . . not to only teach them, but to teach them life skills as well. So that probably includes being literate and being numerate. Because they are the things that's going to drive them later on.

ParklandsT8: Basically, I guess to educate students, I guess socially, and with knowledge to give them the life skills . . . they need to live. Not just like knowledge skills, also giving them life skills to cope out in the world.

The data revealed that many of the teachers (as Willis 1998 had suggested) generally regarded mathematics as a skills base that enabled children to apply such skills in their everyday lives now and in the future. Following are teachers' comments when they were asked about the role of mathematics in their curriculum:

MeadowlandsT8: I think that it [mathematics] is fairly important. It's fundamental, really, as it prepares them for life skills; it is not just teaching maths for the sake of maths. They use a lot of things in daily life.

ParklandsT5: Through the year we would cover all the things that you need to cover to cover the CSF level 2. Throughout the year you would cover everything with an emphasis on number, which would go through the whole year. So number would be in most of your weekly planning, but you might not be doing measurement every week. We probably focus on that in a couple of a weeks a term. It [number] is just consistent throughout the year. You never stop doing number, doing the number aspect of maths.

MeadowlandsT1: Maths as a completely separate subject, because there would be too much that could be lost or go by the wayside. But [it] should be integrated across the curriculum wherever possible. Integration is a secondary consideration.

MeadowlandsT5: I can see that's it's changed since I taught five, six years ago. I can see that it's becoming more practical, and more examples of how children would use it in their everyday life rather than just do these addition problems.

MeadowlandsT9: To give children the opportunity to problem-solve in real-life situations, to develop their concepts about number, and obviously all the other dimensions of maths [space, measurement, chance, and data] so that they are able to use those skills in real life, to give them foundations in the early years. That aspect is important, having the real basics to build on.

This was also mirrored in the responses of the children when we asked them what they thought math was and what they did in math classes:

MPSJ[3]: We do double ones and twos. Learn to count by twos, fives, and tens.

MPSA: Maths is work. We do a lot of things. We do take-aways. [Researcher: "Anything else?"] No.

MPSAd: Work. Play games and count by tens.

MPSM: Games and counting like to 100. Play games and count by tens.

MPSC: Numbers. You count you do sums and take-aways.

However, it was also evident that some teachers related their teaching in math to contemporary times and suggested that we need to include a broader view that included the ability to discuss issues, ideas, and phenomena. For example:

MeadowlandsT6: Just language. Getting to understand the language of maths, not just in maths but even when you do reading and writing, numbers can come up in that. Discussing maths. Numbers and knowing the order of the numbers, dates—the dates, the days, that that's all about time and how we monitor time, and how time goes on, that sort of thing and also maybe even bringing it to the outside [away from school] like when you go to a shop there is maths, for example, or on the street and there is this many cars and that sort of thing. It is more discussion as well as the language.

When asked about the relationship between mathematics and numeracy, teachers replied that they saw numeracy as the applied context for mathematics:

MeadowlandsT1: Numeracy is the glue that sticks the whole thing together. It's a communication tool as well . . . a lot of the things we do without realizing . . . [involve] number. A good background in numeracy leads to dealing with the abstract.

MeadowlandsT9: Numeracy is the big picture, that's what makes us function in the world, and maths is everywhere, and being numerate means that we can plug those maths skills and concepts into our everyday world where they come up incidentally. It gives us our problem-solving foundations, I think. So the maths is the teaching of what we need to be able to function in the world in a numerate way.

ParklandsT2: To be numerate, like to be literate, you have to be able to understand maths and use maths. To be literate means that you can read and you can write. If you can use maths successfully in your life, then you are numerate.

ParklandsT10: I guess I see maths as you are taught the skills and getting them under your belt and in your memory so that when it comes to numeracy, I see numeracy as worldwide, out there in life. If they have been taught the maths and understand the maths, they can go and apply it to different contexts.

Readily evident from the data was that schooling and mathematics in particular were conceptualized as providing contexts in which children could acquire skills that they might be able to apply in real-world contexts now and in their later lives. The use of the word *skills* in our conversations with teachers seemed to encompass both knowledge about content and the ways in which they could and were used. The teachers talked about the content of their curricula in terms of the ways in which it was going to be needed now or later outside of the school context. None of them mentioned tests, in contrast to previous studies (e.g., Yelland 1993), where early childhood teachers in the United Kingdom said they felt pressured to teach content because of the exhaustive national testing regime. This new, applied view of schooling was accompanied by classroom activity that involved a great deal of practicing such skills, based on a belief that children of this age would become competent only if they experienced repetition and repeated use of the skills. Included in this approach were opportunities across the curriculum for children to participate in problem-solving tasks designed to help them to realize the ways in which these skills were going to be useful in authentic contexts. All of the teachers indicated that a primary belief that children learn most effectively by active (hands-on) learning, inquiry (real-world examples), and problem solving (engagement with ideas). A major part of their learning process was promoted by a state-level initiative for organization in literacy and numeracy.

MeadowlandsT8: I do the whole-part-whole [groups] early-years program.

MeadowlandsT11: We follow the Early Years Numeracy Program, where it is whole-part-whole sections. Where you have a shared learning focus on the floor together, you pitch at the middle range of kids in your group and you then send your kids back to do an independent task. You might have a teaching group on the floor that needs a particular focus, whether it is an extension focus or a remedial focus, on that same lesson, and then we have a shared time where we all come back to the floor and discuss what we found out during the lesson.

MeadowlandsT3: We follow the early numeracy approach, that is the whole-part-whole approach. Where you start off with the whole class to explain the focus, then set up activities where I set up teacher group on the floor to further extend the activity, and then they will come together at the end to discuss what was learnt.

MeadowlandsT4: At the start we usually have a focus activity, e.g., might do counting with rolling a dice. Then they might move into individual groups; I might take a small group and assist those that require help with that particular area. Come back together to share what they learned. If they learned something really exciting, then I get them to share it with the class.

MeadowlandsT6: We have a whole group at the start, we share the concept that we are going to talk about, and then they will go off and do an independent activity. There might be some that I will work with, or it might be the whole grade that I work with. It depends on what I am trying to teach and where they are at. And at the end we get together and do a share of what we have learned, or maybe of the strategies that they used, to help them get the answers. We then have a conclusion or summary at the end.

NUMERACY FOR THE TWENTY-FIRST CENTURY

In rethinking the nature of numeracy for the twenty-first century it became increasingly apparent from the literature and from conversations with teachers, principals, and children that a simple conceptualization around the notion of applying skills in everyday life was not effective in encapsulating the significance of such desired abilities. We live in New Times (Hall and Jacques 1989) and function in a data-drenched society (Steen 1999). These times are significantly different from those in which many parents experienced schooling and the application of numeracy skills in their lives, yet they seem to want to return nostalgically to a teaching model in which the basic skills are taught in a mechanistic, rote manner. In the information age new skills that enable individuals to critically interpret and analyze relevant data are foregrounded. Zevenbergen (2004) pointed out that we have moved from an industrial to a technologized society that requires technological, statistical, and economic numeracy to function effectively. These can be used as the framework for numeracies in diverse contexts, which forms the basis of the model presented here.

In this study it was apparent that some teachers were confused about the difference between the terms *mathematics* and *numeracy*, and indeed regarded them as being the same thing. It was felt by some teachers that a new way of thinking about becoming numerate needed to consider not only the use of skills in applied contexts but also the generation of new knowledge as well as a greater depth of understanding about existing knowledge. Further, all the teachers emphasized the need for children to be able to articulate and share ideas, strategies, and findings and that this was an important feature of being numerate. In bringing all these aspects together, the new model for numeracies for the twenty-first century recognized that children needed to use skills and knowledge from all areas in diverse contexts and that they would do this via inquiring, creating, and communicating their ideas and discoveries in all areas of the curriculum. This is represented in Figure 5.1.

The model has three components: inquiry, creation, and communication. In thinking about inquiries that might warrant investigations, both teachers and children will generate ideas and work collaboratively in active learning contexts that require them to use existing knowledge and skills in order to make sense of their world, but additionally will create new knowledge that can be shared with a variety of appropriate

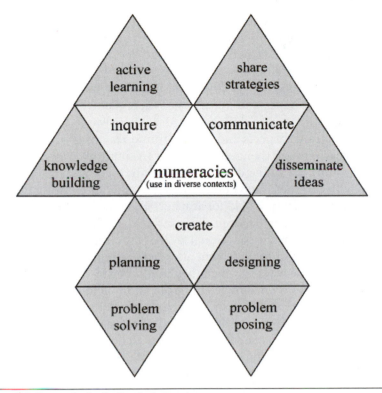

Figure 5.1 Numeracies for the twenty-first century

audiences. This process involves designing, planning, problem posing, problem solving, and then effectively communicating strategies, ideas, and findings to promote new understandings.

Inquiry, creation, and communication flow into one another and are not separate or confined to mathematical contexts. This model, which emerged through talking with the teachers, both reflects their understandings about mathematics and the process of becoming numerate and serves as a point of action for them.

The creation of the model was accompanied by an analysis of the tasks that teachers used in order to provide opportunities for the children in their class to acquire the foundational mathematical skills and knowledge base to use in problem solving (see Appendix 2; for a detailed explanation see Yelland 2005). Although the stated aims of mathematics teaching were to provide the children with the relevant knowledge and skills that they might use in everyday life, in reality most of the time was spent practicing these in very constrained examples. Where there was problem solving it was often in the context of story problems generated by the teacher, with the children required to fig-ure out which operation was needed and then completing the requi-site algorithm. These structured tasks had specific foci and minimal opportunities for exploration. As a consequence, the learning outcomes were limited to specific objectives and behaviors that could be easily demonstrated in paper-and-pencil tests. There seemed to be no time to apply the knowledge and skills acquired, as there was a lot of content to cover. The various aspects and issues around teaching were discussed with the teachers and then represented as an continuum (see Appendix 2) which show the range of ways that children could carry out tasks and activities in the context of mathematics. By representing them on a continuum it was possible for teachers to consider the wide varia-tion that might occur between these tasks and select which were the most appropriate for the conceptual level of the child or relevant for the topic under study. The continuum afforded the opportunity for teach-ers to consider the ways in which they might be able to create learning contexts that would encourage the application of the knowledge and skills via active exploration, inquiry, and problem solving. Multidi-mensional tasks required the open-ended use of mathematical concepts and processes in problem-solving contexts that were characterized by challenging work, sharing strategies, and the use of ICT where relevant and purposeful. In this way the children would be applying their math-ematical knowledge and skills for authentic reasons and in the process becoming numerate. In these extended contexts the children came to realize that there is often more than one solution to a problem, and learning about which one was the most relevant or practical was an important part of the learning process, as was understanding that this sometimes meant coming to a consensus with peers and negotiating an effective outcome. Engaging with such ideas via planned activities meant that the children often took on the responsibility for their own learning after a period of time, having initially been scaffolded by the teacher in order to reach this state of autonomy. This enabled them to grow in confidence as learners, and as a consequence they wanted to learn more and share their ideas with others.

In this way both the model and the continuum became planning frameworks and reflective points for the teachers in the study to think about ways in which the children in their care were becoming numerate. Teachers reported that both of these frameworks (model and contin-uum) were useful for planning purposes, provoking them to think about the ways in which they could create more diverse contexts in which the children in their classes could acquire knowledge and skills that would help them become more effective problem solvers, and also serving as a stimulus for thinking about more challenging tasks that might require more collaborative work for sharing ideas and findings.

When the model and the continuum were used by the teachers in the first year of school, this involved the representation of ideas, with the computer and calculator being possible ways to achieve this. For example, in one task the children were introduced to the concept of division with stories about sharing between people or allocating items to a specific set of containers. In addition to off-computer work reinforcing the concept with manipulatives and writing stories on paper, a computer-based activity linked to the theme of animals was included (see Figure 5.2). This extended the children's thinking at the more difficult level of abstract representation. It has been suggested that computer-based learning in mathematics enables children to make the important transition to abstract thinking by facilitating an inquiry-based approach that requires the use of symbols in dynamic contexts (e.g., Yelland 1999). In this case the children had to read a number story and then allocate fish from a large aquarium to each of three children so that they all had the same number. They were then required to record their findings in a number sentence using the appropriate mathematical language. This could be saved for discussion with the class in the shared session.

At this level of introduction to a new concept within the mathematics curriculum, it was appropriate to make the tasks more structured so

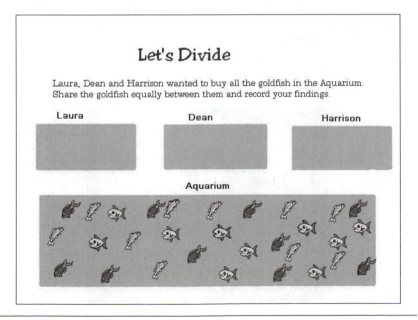

Figure 5.2 The aquarium

that it was possible for the children to demonstrate that they understood the big idea associated with the concept. This focused application enabled them to show their ability to share various items equally among groups, and thus there were limited outcomes in terms of a solution. However, the teacher extended this by creating contexts for learning that required the children to apply the new concept with manipulatives and by writing them with words and numbers (symbols) as well as having the opportunity to manipulate items in two dimensions on the computer screen in order to share them equally. Finally, the aquarium task combined the visual, oral, and symbolic language of mathematics so that the children were able to represent their ideas and share them with the group.

In another example, Amanda was investigating the concept of symmetry. With Kid Pix she was able to draw letters, such as the uppercase *A* shown in Figure 5.3, and then she was able to play with the lines of symmetry of this letter, moving the line and observing the immediate impact of her manipulations on the screen. This dynamic effect would not have been possible without the technology and meant that Amanda was able to realize the consequences of her actions as they were being carried out. Additionally, she could do this for a range of letters in the alphabet and show her results in the form of printouts, which were then available for discussion in the shared session that culminated the investigation of the topic. This task was at an exploratory level of the introduction of the concept, and the teacher included a less structured activity accordingly. It still had specific outcomes in terms of (in this case) finding the line of symmetry, yet it allowed a more open-ended use of examples that could be selected by the children and which

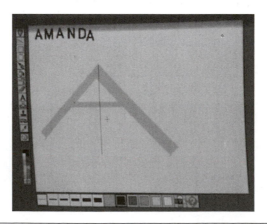

Figure 5.3 Symmetry

enabled them to extend their problem solving and the associated discussion of what they discovered by their own volition. In terms of the continuum from structured use to open-ended use, this task was more open-ended than either the division task or the aquarium task previously described.

In this particular school it was evident that from the first year of school the children were viewed as capable learners. They were encouraged to brainstorm their ideas, reflect on the learning process, and use new technologies as a natural part of their everyday learning across all areas of the curriculum. This often meant following investigations that were project-based, which could stem from an idea initiated by the teacher or the children themselves. For example, in one teacher-initiated project, first graders were required to grow some beans in soil over a period of several weeks and needed to record and document the growth of their beans on a weekly basis. Some of the children chose to represent what they did and observed in Kid Pix, and their drawings then formed part of the class data on the subject of growing beans. This is shown in Figure 5.4, which depicts the three stages in the process. When engaged in this activity the children were able to choose the ways in which they wanted to record and share their ideas about the process. The task was one of the first attempts at documenting and collating information in this way, and they seemed to enjoy it immensely, as demonstrated by their engagement with each other and their conversations around the mathematical ideas inherent to it. This provides an example of a task that is further along the continuum toward being more multidimensional, since there were greater opportunities for self-initiated problem solving and representation of this process as well as the use of a variety of mathematical concepts (e.g., measuring, spatial awareness, use of number, collecting data). Also, the children worked collaboratively and engaged in variable learning processes during the experience. All contributions were regarded as being valuable, and the tasks built on the previous knowledge that the children had acquired in their mathematical classes.

As a final example of moving toward providing opportunities for more multidimensional experiences that enable children to become numerate, groups of children were involved in landscaping their school and creating designs for various parts of the outdoor area. They were required to map the garden beds that had already been planted and consider how they might redesign the areas by adding more plants to further enhance these gardens based on various themed ideas that they had generated. The students measured, mapped, and drew the gardens to scale using rulers, protractors, measuring tapes, and orienteering compasses.

Figure 5.4 Three steps for planting seeds

The maps were designed using Appleworks and featured such ideas as the Grasses Garden, the Entrance Garden, the Pea Garden, and the Bird Garden. The example featured here (Figure 5.5) is the Bird Garden.

When considered in terms of the Mathematical Tasks Continuum in Appendix 2, the garden design task is to a large extent multidimensional in its makeup, as it allows the children to apply various mathematical concepts and processes to create and design a functional garden based on a theme of their choice. When creating the garden, the group was provided with time and resources to investigate the problem of how to create a new garden and conducted research to find out more about native birds and the plants that they would prefer. They represented their ideas using new technologies and were then able to share this with a wide audience beyond the classroom, since the plans were uploaded to the school's Web site. The varied learning outcomes—for example, the different gardens the students created and the ways they approached the task—are multidimensional, as are the multiple opportunities for exploration provided by this task. In addition, students could create their own plant key and represent the scale of the garden within the software, adding to or amending this when required; this provided

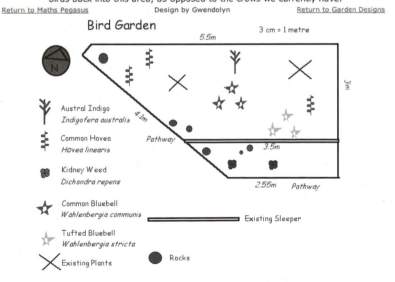

The Bird Garden was designed to attract a number of small native birds that live in our area, into our school. A variety of smaller, bushier species were planted here, to create a good nesting environment for the birds. Plants include varieties of ground covers, wildflowers, small shrubs and medium shrubs. It is hoped that this garden bed, along with the Grasses Bed which is located nearby, will attract the smaller birds back into this area, as opposed to the crows we currently have.

Figure 5.5 The bird garden

the students with multiple opportunities for learning and showing initiative. This task was completed over a series of mathematics classes, allowing for ample time to achieve such worthwhile outcomes and satisfying results.

INTEGRATED LEARNING OPPORTUNITIES

Participation in activities such as these meant that by the time the children were in fifth grade they were able to conduct sustained and coherent investigations on topics such as energy as well as work with the community to gather evidence about the state of a local creek that was becoming polluted. In the energy project these ten-year-olds, working in groups of four, collaboratively researched a history of energy that ranged from moving products with a horse and cart to using wind energy. In this process the group also conducted scientific experiments to illustrate how using a specific style of shower head could conserve water. The children concluded that we needed to reduce our reliance on fossil fuels, which would require citizens to walk and ride bicycles more than use their cars. This information was synthesized into a multimedia presentation using iMovie that incorporated Kid Pix–produced material, a digital camera and movie camera, and scanners. The movie summarized their main findings and was presented to the class for discussion. The interactions provided an opportunity for them to demonstrate the skills that had been deployed during the learning processes as well as the new knowledge that they had acquired during the experience. In this way, they illustrated how they had added to their knowledge base and also the ways in which they generated new solutions. This required a high level of cooperation and the use of creative thinking skills, which we have now come to realize are the basic skills for effective participation in the new century.

In building on this work in the following year, when the children were eleven years old, a larger group conducted a major study of a local river system in order to determine its characteristics and constitutive elements as well as to make recommendations to the local council and community groups about how it might be more effectively managed. This work was made possible by the coherent determination of the teachers in a whole-school approach to integrated learning that enabled the children to build up skills and knowledge as they progressed through the grades. This often meant a great deal of extra work for the teachers involved, since they had to change the way they worked—documenting this learning in new ways and illustrating the specific learning outcomes that were being fostered.

In another school, the children were working on a project entitled Minibeasts, one part of which required them to research and record their minibeasts' various attributes as well as to provide information about the beasts' habitat, life cycle, and food sources. The minibeast topic was a required one in the state education department's science syllabus, but the team of teachers involved decided to innovate on the theme by incorporating the use of the Internet for research purposes. They then extended the children's skill base by teaching them how to do animations as one way in which they might share their findings about minibeasts with each other. The teachers chose this medium of expression because they thought that it would be appropriate and knew it was a skill that the children did not have that might be useful in subsequent school-based project work. The teachers demonstrated the basic components of the process, including the need for a foreground and background, how to take good digital pictures, and the ways in which the clay minibeast that was created for each of the animations would need to be moved for each photograph in order to ensure that the animation was realistic.

The six- and seven-year-old children worked in self-selected groups to make the clay minibeast, create the background and foreground, and set up the animation scene. The teacher organized space to do this and allocated whole-class time to the sharing of strategies so that all the children could learn from the experiences of others regarding the process of creating an animation. This proved to be invaluable—for example, one group realized early on that if they moved the clay animal too far in each step and took only a limited number of digital photos, the animation became disjointed and uneven. Another group had the good idea of using fishing line to move their minibeast so that they could do it in small enough steps for the animation to flow smoothly. Sharing such information made the process much easier and pleasant for the group as a whole. Similarly, at the end of the learning experience each group presented its final animation to the whole class. They shared the new knowledge they had uncovered from their research, and explained the processes they had gone through in order to reach the final products, which were surprisingly varied. One group had chosen to study a spider, and their animation involved the spider going to its web (with a collage web in the background) and eating a fly. One of the members of the group described how they had discussed how best to achieve this in the animation. One had suggested that they could take a bit off the fly each time they took a digital photo, so that it would get smaller and then finally disappear. Another suggestion was to put the fly in the web and move the spider over to cover it a bit at a time so that it would appear as if the spider was eating the fly slowly. She explained

Figure 5.6 Setting up for animations

Figure 5.7 Ladybird minibeast animation

how the group had decided on the second strategy by agreement and how it had worked effectively. She also talked about how they edited the sequence with iMovie, how they had chosen a speed of movement for the slides, and how they came to agree on the final selection.

This project work thus illustrated the ways in which new technologies made a contribution to the knowledge-building process and acted as a medium in which the information that the children had selected could be shared with an audience.

The study revealed that the model provided a context in which the teachers could think about new learning and the ways in which they viewed numeracies for the twenty-first century. The use of the mathematical tasks continuum was valuable as a framework for planning, helping teachers create contexts that supported initial learning with more structured sequences of actions and practice. These could be extended gradually so that the children could successfully take on more responsibility for their own learning in different ways as they became more knowledgeable and skillful.

The realization by the teachers that they should be exposing their children to more diverse tasks reminded me of the early work around gender in which teachers who watched video of their classroom actions did not realize that they were treating boys and girls differently based on their own social expectations until they actually saw it on the tape. In this instance, the teachers who thought that they exemplified constructivist classrooms realized that they needed to think more creatively about aspects of tasks so as to ensure that the children had more opportunities to be responsible for their own learning, as well as participate in tasks that were more open-ended and had multiple paths to solutions.

KIDS OF THE NEW MILLENNIUM

The Children of the New Millennium project, which was introduced in Chapter 2, was also concerned with helping teachers rethink the ways in which they could support and extend children's learning via engagement with ideas and authentic problem solving.

It was based on the premise that it is important to give consideration to semiotics (the study of signs and their systems) and the ways in which meaning is represented in the interpretation of those signs (Lemke 1990; Eco 1990). A consideration of semiotics provides a framework for adopting a broader view of both literacy and numeracy and enables us to think about the underlying processes involved in making meanings derived from graphic symbols. Semiotic analysis recognizes both the cognitive use of symbols by the individual and the social interactions that take place during investigations (Labbo 1996). Additionally, the Children of the New Millennium project drew on the pedagogy of multiliteracies (New London Group 1996), which also recognizes the importance of signs and symbols and how they are used to communicate meanings.

It has already been noted that research about use of ICT with very young children has shown some interesting trends (e.g., Downes and Reddacliff 1996; Labbo 1996). It is evident that the first years of school are a unique time for using computers because this is when children, starting at the ages of four and five years, are developing literacy and numeracy skills as symbolic and graphic meaning makers. They also build concepts and represent meaning for a range of purposes by juxtaposing different symbol systems such as typography, linguistic marks on the page, and symbols on the computer screen.

The Children of the New Millennium project linked preschool teachers and teachers in the early years of school to explore what the current generation of young children can do with ICT, so that this could be connected to their lived experiences in school. The role of the early childhood teacher was viewed as being particularly crucial, since representational skills related to design and construction are required and teachers need to scaffold children's modes of visual thinking (Fleer 2000). This is also the time when the foundations for literacy and numeracy are established (Clay 1993). Knowledge of children's lifeworlds and how they engage with the elements of literacies and numeracies are essential in order to facilitate learning in the early years (Hill et al. 1998). Many early childhood educators lack confidence to engage students with technologies in meaningful ways (Piannfetti 2001). It is apparent, however, not only that teachers have to learn about these new technologies but also that they have to know how to teach using ICT in appropriate ways (e.g., Green, Reid, and Bigum 1999).

One of the teachers participating in the study developed a learning sequence for her third graders around the theme of endangered animals. She had planned the investigation around the notion of resource-based learning, whereby she wanted the children to understand that information could come from a variety of sources—for example, real-world contexts (in this case a visit to a zoo), the Internet, and books in the library. The project started with an organized visit to the local zoo. Prior to the visit the class engaged in a discussion about animals and considered why many cities have zoos. In conversation, one of the things noted was that some zoos do good work by instigating breeding programs for endangered animals, the most famous of which are the pandas. This consideration provided a focus for the zoo visit, and the children were required to think about other animals that are in danger of becoming extinct and thus fulfill the criterion of being endangered. They then chose an animal to study and researched the reasons the animal was under threat. In conducting this investigation the children had to provide information about the animal and what it looked like, the country in which the animal was found, what habitat it thrived in and how it found food. Further, they needed to record their information in varying formats that included note taking and making scientific drawings, and they needed to provide a clear statement of the problem that they were studying.

This was a well-planned investigation by the teacher with a well-defined balance between student autonomy and teacher guidance. The children could choose their topic, and each group decided how they would conduct the research and present their findings. The teacher had objectives related to a recognition that information comes from a variety of sources and that documentation can take various forms. These skills are a valuable component of the research and dissemination process, which is often introduced in the third or fourth year of school to ensure that children have the requisite skills to conduct viable investigations and share their findings with others. This aspect of audience was important, since the children in the study presented their findings to the class, the school, and members of the community. Later, they also created a Web page of their work so that potentially it was available for a worldwide audience.

One group studied the snow leopard, and their work culminated in the presentation of a slide show using Kid Pix. This included both imported photographs of the snow leopard from the Internet and their own (electronic) drawings of the animals. Other children chose to do their illustrations using paints or crayons and then scanned their pictures into the program. Some groups of children included a voice narration of the information they found, while others included text on the relevant pages. The transition from note taking to final product was a collaborative and negotiated process, with each child in the group taking responsibility for various actions. The final products were varied and interesting, illustrating the ways in which the children were able to collate and present their information so that it was transformed into knowledge about the topic they chose. By the end of the unit, the children demonstrated the capacity to complete this group activity, which included a good balance of directed work and autonomous learning that ensured that each project was different yet contained certain elements that were illustrative of good research practices and presentation format. Furthermore, later in the year they

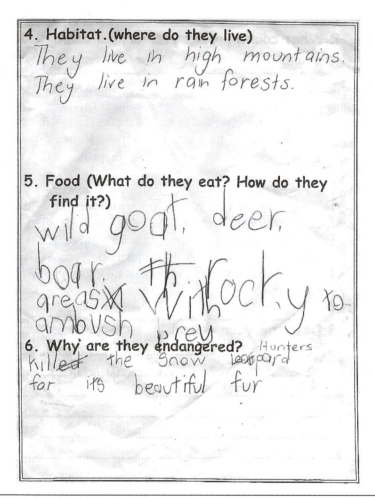

Figure 5.8 Researching the snow leopard

organized a cake-and-jam stall at the school fair to raise money for a donation to the World Wildlife Fund so that they could support the giant panda program.

In conducting these projects it became apparent that the children were using their mathematical ability as well as demonstrating that they could be effective researchers and produce a coherent final product that adhered to certain conventions for effective communication. Thus they showed that they were able to be numerate in these contexts. For example, they used numbers in their reporting—one project included a graph indicating which animals were most vulnerable to becoming

Figure 5.9 The habitat of the snow leopard

extinct. Additionally, their spatial awareness was used in the design of their slide show layout, and their knowledge about time zones in the various areas under investigation was extended.

These examples provide a stark contrast to governments' proposals for the use of new technologies for learning (most often referred to in terms of "online content"). In Australia, for example, large amounts of government funding have been devoted to the production of "learning objects" as the basic form of online content. The actual objects are, of course, varied in type and quality, but on the whole they are exemplified by what happened in the United States when educational computer software first came on the market. As Negroponte (1995) stipulated:

> In the 1960s, most pioneers in computers and education advocated a crummy drill-and-practice approach, using computers on a one-on-one basis, in a self-paced fashion, to teach those same God-awful facts more effectively. Now, with multimedia, we are faced with a number of closet drill-and-practice believers, who think they can colonize the pizazz of a Sega game to squirt a bit more information into the thick heads of children. (Negroponte 1995, 198–199)

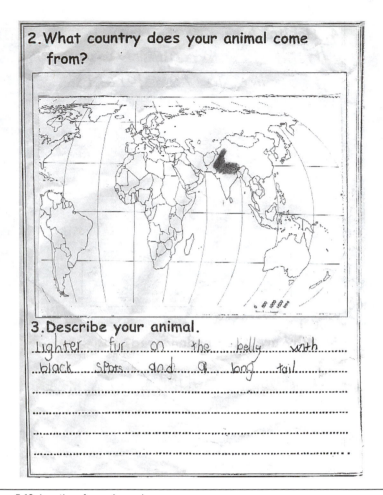

Figure 5.10 Location of snow leopards

Many examples of digital learning objects are now available to teachers on CD-ROMs. A catalogue of items and some samples are available online (see Learning Federation 2005). In reviewing these learning objects it is immediately obvious that they are designed to reinforce existing curricula and teaching with electronic pizazz. They seem to be designed for individual use and minimal teacher intervention; it is difficult to think of ways in which children might use them to share their findings and strategies to support further learning. In the introduction to the mathematics and numeracy learning objects section the catalogue stated:

The learning objects make use of the digital environment in innovative ways to enhance student learning. For example, some objects allow teachers to set up learning opportunities in mathematics that are normally too complex in a standard classroom; others allow students to visualise and apply mathematics concepts in new ways; others provide opportunities for repeated use by students through randomisation of learning activities; relevant and authentic contexts for exploration and skill application are a feature of others. Scaffolding of student learning and feedback in various multimodal formats are incorporated in all the learning objects. (Learning Federation 2005, 5)

These are worthy goals, but it is difficult to see how they are achieved with the examples that are provided for teachers in the current batch of offerings. One learning object under the topic "Number: Exploring Number" is called "Number Trains" and is intended for use by children from five to eight years of age. The instructions advise: "Make a train of four carriages. Each carriage must be one number bigger than the one before it. Start by putting this carriage on any of the tracks below." The notes that accompany the catalogue advise teachers that this learning object can be used for a range of number work under five separate headings: whole numbers to 10, whole numbers to 20, whole numbers from 30 to 50, whole numbers from 90 to 120, and finally skip counting (by twos, fives, and tens). It is not clear why the numbers from 21 to 29 or from 51 to 89 are omitted. The way in which the information is presented makes it clear that the intention is that these are separate categories in a developmental sequence and that since the children doing the activity only have to put four numbers in sequence, the range of numbers should be limited. Specifically, for each category the same text is used, except the range of numbers is changed. For example:

Number trains: whole numbers to 10. Students place train carriages on a track in order, one at a time, by working out the number that comes before and after the number on each carriage of whole numbers to 10. Numbers are represented as words, numerals and dots that represent quantities. (Learning Federation 2005, 6)

This type of task has been in mathematics curricula for a long time. I can recall doing a similar activity in primary school before 1960, from a textbook with ready-made pictures, instead of it being on a computer screen, and recall my daughters doing this type of number sequencing when they first started school in 1990. It is important to know number names, the associated numerals, their sequence, what they represent, and how they are related to each other. In fact, *Sesame Street* effectively deals with this topic with sophisticated visual images accompanied by oral information for their audience of preschool children. This particular learning object constitutes what I would call busywork. It is hardly engaging, even on a computer, and never challenging. It simply keeps children occupied doing work that has been deemed essential to the curriculum for as long as we can all remember. I would question the need to spend vast amounts of money on creating a dedicated learning object for this concept. It does not really require the use of technology except in an attempt to glitz up content that could be dealt with adequately in conversation, or within the context of counting for a real purpose, such as naming and numbering children in a line for a fire drill or on a class excursion to ensure that no one is missing.

In the same catalogue there is another example of a number activity designed to teach the commutative property of addition. Specifically, it seems to be related to filling in the missing addend in addition algorithms. Three numbers, 18, 16, and 2, are presented on the screen. They are placed on colored bars so that the 18 is at the top, and immediately beneath it are the 2 and 16 on the same size bar. However, it is easy to be distracted from this since the numerals are quite large and cover the single units that make up the bars of 18, and the numerals themselves are not positioned to emphasize the relationship between them. The important idea to view in this visual representation is that 2 and 16 together make 18. The algorithm to represent this is presented below the diagrams to read: $16 + \Delta = 18$. If the child types in 2, there is immediate feedback to indicate that this is the correct answer. If the child doesn't answer correctly, the child get two more turns before the correct answer is given with a written explanation. It should be noted that only one of the learning objects that I have viewed has sound incorporated into it. This is strange since all the computer and video games on the market today are quite sophisticated. When no sound accompanies the visuals, it makes the learning objects seem somewhat unsophisticated in comparison. Once again, it would seem that what happens in schools is a poor reflection of what is available in the commercial world outside it. This is despite the fact that the development of the learning objects probably cost as much, if not more, than commercially developed educational games (they are available at no cost to teachers; thus there is no financial return on the products).

On viewing and trialing other learning objects related to the area of a triangle, patterns, the shape maker, and one in the "Innovation, Enterprise and Creativity" section called Fish Market, it is readily apparent that they all represent examples of mapping new technologies onto old curricula and do not adhere to the stated objectives of the scheme. What is even more problematic is that when a comparison is made between the amount of money invested and the time needed to complete each of the activities, it would seem as if the money spent is not worth it. No one seems to have asked, "How can we do things differently because of this new technology?" As a consequence, digital content does not reflect an exciting new direction for learning but rather reinforces old learning in an expensive and perhaps unproductive way.

SUMMARY

This chapter has explored the ways in which new learning can be enacted in schools and has provided examples, with specific reference to becoming numerate in the twenty-first century. A contemporary view of numeracy was presented as a model that highlighted the need for a broader conceptualization of the notion in New Times. In this model the three components are inquiry, creation, and communication. The model provides a framework for teachers to consider the ways in which they provide contexts for children to become numerate, and when used in conjunction with a mathematical tasks continuum the model enabled them to ensure that explorations could be initiated by the teacher or the children and that there were sufficient benefits. The main issues related to providing opportunities for skill and knowledge building in environments characterized by a range of pedagogies that incorporated the use of new technologies, which resulted in deep learning by children.

NOTES

1. ARC Discovery Grant DP0211777. Grieshaber, Yelland. "Becoming Numerate with ICT."
2. In this section teachers are identified by school pseudonyms (Meadowlands & Parklands) and numbered as T1, T2, et cetera, to distinguish between them.
3. Here the pseudonyms are abbreviated to initials: Meadowlands (M) and the first letter in the student's name (e.g., J, A, Ad, M, and C).

6

NEW LEARNING IN THE THIRD MILLENNIUM

The more things change, the more they stay the same.

—*French proverb*

Education can make a difference in people's quality of life. Certainly, as was stated at the start of this book, governments around the world promote education as the main key for economic success. Political leaders deliver speeches about the ways in which their citizens will lead more fruitful lives as a result of their initiatives in education. Yet simultaneously they pander to the results of international test comparisons, which focus on the aspects of education that have the least to do with being effective in the twenty-first century, that is, rote learning and memorization.

As noted, such skills might have been useful in an industrial era that required workers to perform simple, routine, and mundane functions without question, but they are increasingly less important in contemporary times. In fact, for a very long time school systems have performed the social function of sorting students for society so that they could get an education that suited their clearly defined station in life. In the 1970s Illich (1971) produced a powerful critique to illustrate and analyze the ways in which education systems as manifested in schools maintain social order and reproduce social systems that suited the needs of an industrial society. Freire (1972) wrote about the ways in which a liberatory form of education could be created that would empower individuals and lead to a more egalitarian state. So while it is recognized that new forms of teaching and learning are needed for the new era, many school systems seem to value and promote old learning and the associated out-comes related to the possession of specific and privileged knowledge.

This book has questioned this educational focus and noted that despite it appearing as if schools are in a perpetual state of reform (Cuban 2001), we have a long way to go to ensure that schools provide children with educational opportunities that are suited to the needs of New Times. It has considered specific examples of the ways in which systems have reconceptualized curricula and pedagogies. It has described scenarios from a variety of empirical research studies to illustrate the learning that has taken place and how this enables children to become engaged, collaborative, and productive learners in New Times. The learning sce-narios have incorporated the use of new technologies that have essen-tially transformed our lives over the past two decades but which have had minimal impact on changing what goes on in schools. More than that, they are used in a context characterized by authentic learning in knowledge-building communities, so that children are able to build up skills for learning across their lifeworlds and for lifelong learning. Thus, this book has promoted the belief that new technologies should not only change the *ways* that students in schools can learn but also afford opportunities for them to increase the range of knowledge and ideas that are accessible so that they are able to participate in knowledge processing rather than merely be consumers of facts.

The use of new technologies is frequently derided on the basis that their use will be harmful to children or that they will come to rely on the machines too much and lose skills that are still regarded as founda-tional learning. For example, children are made to write stories using pencils and paper because we don't have enough computers and they need to know how to type before they can use a word processor effec-tively. But as Hitchins stated, "There is only one argument for doing something; the rest are arguments for doing nothing" (2001, 43).

CREATIVITY AND INNOVATION IN TWENTY-FIRST-CENTURY EDUCATION

In recognizing that new technologies have transformed all aspects of our lives and influenced the sphere of work, as demonstrated in a shift from labor-intensive industrial industries to a knowledge economy, it is increasingly apparent that flourishing cultures and economies require workers to be creative, to be innovative, and to have high levels of specialist knowledge (Robinson 2001).[1] As a consequence, govern-ments and businesses in developed countries have acknowledged that the key to a successful economic transition lies in education, producing students who work well in collaborative contexts and are creative, innovative, and flexible. Social and economic imperatives underpin the international push for educators to teach students to be creative thinkers and innovators. Increasingly, a competitive edge is based on knowledge, creativity, and innovation rather than land, labor, and capital (e.g., Amabile 1988; Beeman 1990). Innovation accounts for more than half the economic growth in the United States and Britain (McCreedy 2004), and in fact the British seem to be leading the way in terms of initiatives in education on creativity and creative partnerships (Department for Culture, Media, and Sport 2001). The British education secretary calls this the "learning age of creativity, enterprise and scholarship," and Prime Minister Tony Blair has noted that Britain is a nation "living by its wits" (Craft, Jeffrey, and Leibling 2001).

Accordingly, to compete in the global economy, countries need to invest in educating citizens so that they are able to demonstrate the capacity to be innovative, creative, inventive, entrepreneurial, and enterprising. Creativity and innovation in particular need to become central to the educational process. In fact, creativity and innovation should be regarded as foundational workplace skills in a knowledge economy together with becoming adept in information management, self-organization, interdisciplinary capability, emotional intelligence, risk management, and reflective and evaluative capabilities. Furthermore, creative and innovative individuals will be able to adjust more readily to a world that is increasingly complex, one that often lacks job security and requires lifelong learning to keep up with rapid workplace and technological changes (National Advisory Committee on Creative and Cultural Education 1999). Being creative and innovative enables individuals to be more effective citizens and workers who can adapt to changing circumstances (Craft 2001).

Importantly, it has been shown that creativity and having opportunities to be innovative enhance the educational process by actively engaging students in the learning process. They subsequently view school as a place for discovery, openness to new ideas, independent learning, and exploration with others (Loveless 2003). Creativity and the capacity to be innovative require well-structured learning environments and fluency with certain knowledge domains, along with a delicate balance between student-driven inquiry and teacher feedback and intervention. They also involve a design process in which ideas are shaped, refined, and managed to achieve purposive outcomes. This in turn requires perseverance, sustained hard work, and the purposive application of knowledge and skills to enable new connections to be made (National Advisory Committee on Creative and Cultural Education 1999).

There has been some recognition in Australia of the significance of creativity and innovation. In the Australian state of Victoria there is a strong policy mandate in the Victorian Essential Learning Standards, with their interdisciplinary strands of design, creativity, and technology and their focus on engagement with the processes of designing, constructing, and evaluating as a way of stimulating creativity and innovation. This is exemplified by the recognition that design is a "vital step in transforming ideas into creative, practical and commercial realities by optimising the value of products and systems" (Victorian Curriculum and Assessment Authority 2005, 4). In South Australia the Essential Learnings Capabilities place value on critical thinking, risk taking, providing contexts for imagination and creativity, and the ability to generate ideas (Department of Education and Children's Services 2001). The stated goals are for learners to develop a sense of power, creativity, wisdom, and enterprise and the capability to critically evaluate, plan, and generate ideas and solutions. Australian employers have expressed a strong preference for employees with creativity and flair, as they are needed to enable firms to compete globally This places new demands on Australian schools, for "[r]aising academic standards alone will not solve the problems we face. . . . To move forward we need a fresh understanding of intelligence, of human capacity and of the nature of creativity" (Robinson 2001, 9).

This suggested focus on creativity and innovation also adds to the existing educational literature on multiliteracies (Cope and Kalantzis 2000; New London Group 1996), which has been described and illustrated in the chapters in this book. It also complements the work done on providing educational contexts to support multiple intelligences, which understands that students have diverse interests, different learning styles, and need varied literacies for different contexts (Gardner 2000). Engagement with the lifeworlds of students, characterized by sharing perspectives and expanding horizons of knowledge, is a starting point for developing multiple perspectives, taking risks, and exploring self-initiated projects. This pluralist approach to education is supported by Richard Florida's study showing that diversity and tolerance of difference attract the "creative class," who are central to the economic prosperity of certain regions and cities (Florida 2003). Consequently, an education system that respects diversity in the classroom is more likely to provide stimulus for economic development, along with positive social outcomes.

The economic imperative that requires creative workers also necessitates that we provide new ways of teaching students how to be creative thinkers for the twenty-first century. This requires consideration of student-centered learning with group projects, as well as the facilitation of self-directed learning activities that are derived from authentic problem posing and problem solving by the students. Knowledge-building processes are fundamental to these learning contexts, and monitoring outcomes becomes even more important. It has been suggested that the creative and innovative person requires self-confidence, discipline, mastery of a given domain, self-evaluation, risk taking, questioning, and imaginative ways of thinking (Csikszentmihalyi 1996). This is unlikely to be encouraged in a traditional classroom with a teacher talking at passive students and presenting ideas in ways that are definitive and unambiguous (Cazden 2001).

THE BACKLASH: "BACK TO BASICS" AND "NO CHILD LEFT BEHIND"

Those who support the back-to-basics approach (e.g., Donnelly 2006) seem to think that the statement and enactment of such imperatives are a major threat to the very foundation of the educational systems in the Western world. In advocating for a back-to-basics stance, the lobbyists who purport to have children's and society's welfare as a priority are lamenting the ability of students who cannot perform what they regard as simple tasks: the inability to spell common or frequently used words, either orally or in a pencil-and-paper context, operating (e.g., adding, subtracting, dividing, or multiplying) on two- or three-digit numbers without a calculator, and reading "classic" texts and answering specific questions to show their comprehension of such texts. In addition, they require that children be able to generate their own texts so that they are able to be understood, via the use of appropriate grammatical conventions of the language. Additionally, they have a prescribed set of content, traditionally organized as subject matter, that they deem as essential to all, which needs to be learned by rote and regurgitated in tests or under examination conditions. More recently in Australia, knowing the names of the prime ministers from federation onward has been included in this list of essential knowledge (Dapin 2006). The application of such skills and information in real-world contexts rarely receives a mention; rather, the focus is on the demonstrated capacity of students to reproduce the actions and facts under controlled conditions. Implicit in such a focus is the idea that if a child is capable of doing this, then the child must *know* the material. What the back-to-basics supporters do not clearly articulate is the extent to which imbuing and practicing for these skills and remembering the "stuff" functions as education; nor do they address whether students in schools should actually do anything with this "stuff" in an applied way. They also deride educational reforms on the basis that that they ignore "the basics" and inculcate a laissez-faire system in which children are virtually free to do what they want and express themselves while ignoring the conventions of acceptable communication systems. This type of blatant misrepresentation is most typically conducted in the context of literacy, where the whole-language approach, which encourages the use of language in context, is contrasted with the so-called phonics approach, which drills the basic sound and letter combinations that underpin many of the words in the English language and is then supported with a look-and-say approach for the many words that are not phonetically structured. English happens to be a language in which a knowledge of phonics is useful for those starting out to learn. It should, of course, be supplemented with a whole range of strategies for remembering or figuring out (written) words that defy working out but are useful to remember. There are forty-four phonemes (basic speech sounds) in English and twenty-six letters of the alphabet. It should not be difficult to teach these in a systematic and meaningful way in order to assist children to build up a repertoire of skills that they acquire for a purpose that is evident to them. This should not be in the form of drilling a sound or two a week during the school year and practicing them on worksheets. Gee (2004) has noted that young children who play with Pokémon cards with their friends demonstrate outstandingly complex understandings of up to thousands of characters who interact with each other in a myriad of ways. Thus they are capable not only of recognizing and working with combinations but also of remembering them and using them accurately and effectively. The whole-language approach *can* incorporate the teaching of phonics in context as well as the spelling and recognition of many of the words that we want to use to express our ideas. Those who advocate a whole-language approach, or learning language in context, believe that fluency and proficiency are acquired and consolidated when language is encountered and used frequently and as the need arises. Language work has to have a connection and purpose that is clear to the learner; otherwise it will not be meaningful, connected to their lives, and used when appropriate. This is very different from learning skills in isolation via superficial worksheet examples. In the former context the use of language for authentic purposes will encourage a love of books and engagement with ideas. If skills are taught in isolation, not only are the tasks tedious, but they often provide no way for children to make connections between them and their daily lives. This is clearly illustrated in the following example, where a child in his first year of school experiences the literacy hour every day of each school term.

The literacy hour was introduced so that young learners in the first three years of school could be equipped with the literacy skills that would enable them to function effectively and be deemed to be on the road to literacy. During the literacy hour in Victoria, which often extends for a session of one and a half or two hours, children are allocated to groups based on their ability as defined in screening tests and observation-based evaluations, and they rotate around three or four activities during this period. The sessions typically begin with the whole class seated on a carpet while the teacher explains all the activities that they will participate in before they go back to their desks to complete them in the prescribed sequence of activities for the group. One of the goals of the literacy hour is for the teacher to work with a small group for one of the activities so that s/he is able to have uninterrupted time teaching a particular skill and provide individual attention to those who might need it. The activities included are usually structured so that the children practice a skill that has already been introduced to the whole group, and are based on the notion that young children need to consolidate such skills in order for them to be internalized and understood. On one particular day in a classroom I made the following observations about the literacy hour, which was recorded in the teacher's planning schedule as "learning center activities."

Student names were shown on the board as being allocated to one of four groups: orange, yellow, green, and pink. A child was put in charge of each group and called the "leader." The teacher gathered the children together to sit on the mat, and she explained each of the activities.

1. *Read and draw.* This exercise explored the letter *L*. The worksheet was divided into eight parts, each of which depicted a different illustration accompanied by the word label for it: *ball, lamb, ladder, car, lion, mule, shop,* and *lollipop.* The children were to write their names on the top of the sheet and then trace over the letter *L* in lower- and uppercase on separate lines just below the space for their names. The children were then required to circle all the things beginning with *L* (sounded out in the whole-group context), and when they finished this they were told to color all the pictures on the sheet. The instruction "Circle all the things that start with *L*" was written on the sheet.
2. *Computer center.* On the computer was a phonics program called Lily Loves Lollipops. A short animation sequence was shown, and then the children were required to click on the

items that begin with *L*: *lady, lantern, lock, loaf, loop* (in a rope), *leaf, lemon, light*. These are interspersed randomly with non-*L* items such as *bird, bell, dog, cat,* and many more.

3. *Activity table.* Each child was provided with the materials to make the letter *L* out of play dough, and then add some other play dough letters to make words.

4. *Teaching group.* The teacher and group read a book called *Wings,* after which the children had to find images of various items as instructed by the teacher (e.g., bat wings) and discuss the types of animals that have wings and those that don't as well as add to the list of things with wings that were not included in the book. The group then took out their own (exercise) books and wrote a sentence together with a picture to illustrate the sentence.

I remained with the read-and-draw group doing the *L* worksheet. One boy (age five years, in his first term of compulsory schooling) completed the sheet immediately (within a minute) and then just sat there looking at his group. I was talking to another child but then went over to him. At first glance, his worksheet contained black crayon scribbles all over each box. This had the effect of nearly covering each item, so it was hard to recognize them, and seemed to indicate that he had not completed the task effectively, as requested. I asked him which things on the sheet started with *L*. He immediately replied, "Lamb, ladder, lion, and lollipop." I asked why he had not circled them but had colored each of the items. He said that he had circled them, and on inspection I saw that under the black crayon scribbles there was indeed a circle for each of the *L* items. So then I asked why all the boxes were colored black, and he replied, "'Cause the teacher said when you are finished you have to color them all in!" I then asked him if any of the items ended with *L*. He glanced down at the paper and replied: "Yes, there is one—ball." I said, "Can you think of any other words that end with *L*?" He thought for a minute or so, then said: "*Bull, full, hill, bill, . . .* and *. . . kill.*" I wrote them down on the back of the sheet as he said them. I was worried in case this was not the usual protocol, but given his performance with the black crayon on the sheet I got the impression he was not concerned about neatness. As I wrote them and as he finished his list, he asked why all the words that end in *L* have two *L*s. I said I was not sure, and he asked me if words with *L* in the middle, such as *lollipop*, also always had two *L*s as well, and we went on to think about these, name them, and write them down.

I use this example to illustrate the ways in which young children will become disengaged with learning in schools. If I had not been in the class on this occasion, this child would probably have sat there for the twenty-five minutes allocated to this task either doing nothing or, as I found out later, perhaps causing disruption to others. It is my contention that this simplistic task had no potential to engage the child in learning without the associated interactions that went on with it. Further, neither did any of the activities in the session. The tokenistic use of the computer was perhaps the worst-case scenario, since it involved using the machine to reinforce a bad activity that did not need to be completed with a new technology at all. By the time the rotation was over it was apparent that this young learner was adept in recognizing things that start with *L*. It was also evident in my conversation with him that he could generate, from his own vocabulary, more words that started with the letter as well as those that ended with it and had one or two in the middle. In a later rotation he also revealed that he could construct sentences orally at a more extensive rate than when having to write them, which is a frequent observation in preparatory or kindergarten classrooms. However, in discussion with the teacher I was told that he "had learning problems and needed extra literacy classes with the special needs teacher . . . and he is disruptive to others when working." I could see how she came to this conclusion in reviewing his work, which looked unattractive and provided little evidence of competence. Unless you talked to him you would not know that he understood the concept being practiced, but what I was not prepared for was the lack of opportunity this busy and competent teacher had to talk with him to explore what competencies he did have that could be built on.

REVITALIZING SCHOOLING

Two questions in particular arise out of the literacy hour scenario. First, why are we doing these type of activities? Second, what is the alternative? There is no doubt in my mind that to be a successful communicator and meaning maker in the English language individuals need to know certain things, such as phonics as a strategy for decoding and recognizing specific words. Additionally, they need to have experiences in building up proficiency in reading with books designed specifically to inculcate these skills as well as working with a range of other reading materials and literary experiences, such as reading signs, logos, and electronic texts, discussing advertisements, and viewing films and having the opportunity to discuss them. Simultaneously, young children need authentic experiences of their own choosing as well as by design of the teacher that enable them to use these skills in action for extended periods of time. Education should be more than just "covering stuff" that is deemed to be important from an industrial frame of reference and doing activities that involve continual repetition and demonstration of skills that children are already accomplished in.

Those who are interested in making education relevant for the twenty-first century, such as myself, do not contend that children can embark on project-based investigations unless they have some fundamental and basic skills that will support the methods of inquiry and communication of the findings. I would suggest that these can be introduced and used in context and that young children should not have to, for example, study a sound or a number for a week and fill in mindless worksheets in order to have a record of the fact that it has been "covered." How many times does a child have to complete a worksheet on adding up sums to prove that s/he can add? Recently, in Australia, the use of calculators was banned from final-year school exams, and their use in class time was also vastly reduced. The reasons cited related to the fact that many pupils were using calculators for "everything," including simple sums such as 4 + 2. No evidence was provided to support this claim, but it missed the fundamental point that calculators remove the necessity for routine and mechanical computation. They do not reduce the need for understanding computation and when it needs to be used. However, given what calculators can do, their presence should impact on the quality and type of mathematical experiences in school. For example, there is a decreased need to study long division as a result of calculators, and graphics calculators have changed the very nature of graphing work currently practiced in the early secondary years of schooling. To make students take exams to demonstrate their competence in a context of "no calculators" not only is naive, in that it sets schools up as places that don't use the everyday materials available in the outside world in the twenty-first century, but also separates out school and identifies it as a place that requires skills that have no relevance to students' lives. Papert has suggested that such people should be called "cyber ostriches," since they

> can only imagine using them [computers] in the framework of the school system as they know it. . . . This is quite perverse: new technology being used to strengthen a poor method of education that was invented only because there were no computers when school was designed. (1996, 25)

In contrast to these narrow views of schooling, this book has provided examples of children working and learning in schools in contexts that were designed to promote deep learning and the use of skills in authentic contexts. There are also other examples of the fine work being done in rich educational settings that encourage children to work individually and collaboratively so that they are building knowledge and participating in investigations that have real purposes.

SCIENCE TALKS

Karen Gallas (1995) has shown that it is possible for five- to eight-year-olds to engage in productive discussions about complex issues that they have generated as questions. In providing a learning environment that she has called Science Talks, children were able to explore their questions and ideas with her as their teacher and also with community members who have specialized knowledge. The starting point for the Science Talks is usually a question, and at the beginning of the process Gallas advises teachers to construct one such as "Why do leaves change color?" The role of the teacher in the talks is fluid but can best be characterized as that of a facilitator. The teacher listens to the talks and initially provides commentary, makes a summation, and asks new questions about statements the children have made. Gradually, the children become adept at organizing their own talks, and although the teacher is present and involved, the ownership and organization of the talks becomes the responsibility of the group of children. With years of experience, Gallas has noted that the most effective questions are open-ended and may have multiple answers. Initially, the children tended to ask specific questions such as "Who made the first clock?" which, while interesting, did not afford as much opportunity for extended discussion as the more open-ended questions. Her book is filled with wonderful dialogues of young children debating ideas and issues and questions such as: "What is blood for?" "Why is the ocean salty?" "How did the moon begin?" But they did not just talk. They also recorded their findings and presented them to the whole group in order to share what they had discovered and direct the discussion to a new level of inquiry or investigation. In the process they became theory builders, just like scientists in the real world.

A FOCUS ON IDEAS AND
NEW KNOWLEDGE CREATION

The notion that what we do in schools and how curricula are enacted as tasks and activities has been challenged by Scardamalia, who contended that:

The target of true 21st-century education should be the advanced knowledge processes that scientists, scholars, and employees of highly innovative companies engage in daily. These processes must be built into the social fabric of communities, and into the technologies that support their work, so that creative knowledge work is as integral to schooling as it is to our most high-powered knowledge-creating organizations. (2005, 1)

On the basis of her extensive studies, Scardamalia identifies the sociocognitive dynamics of knowledge building as including the *knowledge processes* of direct engagement with problems of understanding, work with emergent rather than fixed goals, evolution of goals toward higher-level formulations of problems, self-organization around promising new directions rather than mandated work on other-directed and scripted activities, work at the edge of competence, self-monitoring and self-correction without undue dependence on external evaluation, engagement with knowledge-intensive processes that lead deeper into the field of inquiry, productive use of idea diversity, risk taking, and responsibility for high-level sociocognitive activities such as setting and refining goals, providing resources, and identifying different perspectives (Scardamalia 2005, 1–2).

That schools should be places where new knowledge is generated should not be a revolutionary idea. Our culture is one that is built on creativity and innovation in all endeavors; this starts from the beginning of life and should continue in schools. Currently, the focus on routine or mundane tasks is the complete antithesis of this but is justified in terms of the need for young children to acquire and practice skills and knowledge. Curricula organized around disciplines and subjects perpetuate this situation and mean that tasks to instill skills and knowledge are the main form of activity. Subject and discipline specialists then carefully guard their domains with the associated knowledge sets for fear of their subject being relegated or discarded in the name of reform. Consequently, usually nothing is taken away from curricula, but more is added, and we end up with overcrowded curricula.

Recent trends in the sciences have meant that at the university level, at least, there has been a desire for students to integrate subject matter and skills across the range of biological sciences to include those from the health sciences and even from the traditional arts subjects such as anthropology. The justification and defense of secondary curricula have usually been rallied around the needs of universities, even though many students do not proceed to higher education. However, it would seem that changes in the university system have the potential to impact on the traditional subjects, that will be taught in secondary schools since they might become redundant. In the elementary and early years there is no reason why a focus on ideas and investigations should not be at the core of education in a context where skill acquisition, knowledge building, and the generation of new knowledge are primary goals. The work of Scardamalia (2003, n.d.) and Gallas (1995, 2003) provides examples of the ways in which *ideas* rather than routine *tasks* can be the focus of curricula, particularly in the early years of schooling (though there is evidence to show that it will be successful in later years as well).

NEW TECHNOLOGIES, NEW PEDAGOGIES, NEW LEARNING

Already the emergence of new technologies has presented challenges to rethink pedagogical practices and reexamine the traditional classroom environment (Chadler-Olcott and Mahar 2003; Yelland 2005). They have enabled educators to think more about strategies for learning and discovery rather than about privileged "stuff to know," so that it is more important to know *how to learn* than to know the names of presidents in chronological order or being able to instantly recall the product of 6 and 7. The ways in which new technologies are embedded into pedagogies and learning are essential to the processes of creativity and the ability to be innovative (Loveless 2003; Yelland 1999, 2002c).

It is apparent that teachers need to understand the implications of all these issues for their classroom practice and pedagogies so that they are able to make effective decisions about curriculum, process, and assessment. This book has attempted to share some of the ways in which this might be achieved. It has explored the potential of new technologies as means of investigating, exploring, representing, communicating, and sharing ideas. It has not been my purpose here to provide examples in which new technologies have been used to support old learning. Neither have I advocated for technology-based learning scenarios that simply use machines as tools. In fact, the presence of the technologies should be subsidiary to the exploration of ideas and the creation of new understandings. So often one reads about the need to justify spending on computers in schools in terms of improved outcomes. Unfortunately, such outcomes are usually limited to test scores, and the tests themselves do not incorporate the use of computers in any way at all. This is very strange but understandable in some ways, since it is difficult to measure the nature of the influence and impact that new technologies might have on learning.

Computers and other new technologies enable us to think differently and experience phenomena in new and varied dimensions. They also allow access to and experiences with ideas that would not normally have been encountered prior to their use. They afford new contexts for learning in the early years, together with a range of other new technologies, such as cameras and other peripherals, that have the potential to enhance young children's experiences and understandings about the world and complement the use of other resources available. They represent one form of resource and need to be selected when appropriate; they highlight the need for creative thought and innovative ideas so that we are able to benefit from their application. This book has presented examples to show what is possible, and I hope it will act as a catalyst for action.

NOTE

1. This section is adapted from the ARC Linkage Application LP0669066 (Yelland, O'Rourke, Loveless with Wardlaw), "Backing our Creativity: Raising the Bar for Excellence in Student Achievement."

7

WHERE NEXT? SUPPORTING LEARNING AND UNDERSTANDING LEARNERS IN THE TWENTY-FIRST CENTURY

Dr. Kerry Wardlaw

Victoria University, Melbourne, Australia

INTRODUCTION

Following on from the themes raised throughout this book, this chapter provides examples of some Web-based sources and information that follow the structure of topics in the preceding chapters. Some resources do not fit specifically within one given chapter, since the book's themes are interrelated. The first chapter, "The Millennials," addresses the ways policy makers and researchers recognize that new technologies are an important part of children's daily life and need to be integrated into schooling. "New Contexts for Learning" explores positive examples of pedagogies and curricula that integrate new technologies. "Making Meaning: Technology as Play" gives examples of play as learning facilitated by digital toys and digital software. "Thinking and Knowing: Informal Learning at Home and in Communities" discusses learning experiences that show a potential direction for creating new learning environments in schools and different approaches to organizing classroom dynamics. There are also examples of innovations in school environments in the chapter "New Ways of Learning in School." They include not only transforming pedagogies but also reassessing what we consider to be foundational skills. The concluding chapter, "New Learning in the Third Millennium," points to future directions by drawing on the work of researchers who suggest new models for schooling that integrate new technologies, and alternative schools that have already paved the way in terms of an emphasis on creativity, child-centered learning, and more flexible spaces and social interactions.

THE MILLENNIALS

Policy makers and educators increasingly recognize that there is a need to integrate ICT more effectively into education contexts in order to equip students for a world of rapid technological, social, and economic change. Children of the new millennium grow up in a media-saturated technoculture, and schools are increasingly required to adapt pedagogies and curriculum content in order to engage this tech-savvy generation in learning. This section of resources shows a shift in education toward at least recognizing the importance of integrating ICT into education. However, despite this recognition, there has been a tendency to merely add new technologies without rethinking curriculum and pedagogy. Furthermore, there are still some organizations, such as the Alliance for Childhood, that are antagonistic to integrating new technologies into early childhood and primary education.

Kaiser Family Foundation

The Kaiser Family Foundation Web site (http://www.kff.org) has major studies on media use by youth. The latest publication is "Generation M: Media in the Lives of 8–18-Year-Olds" (March 2005), which updates research from a 1999 study, "Kids and Media @ the New Millennium." Both surveys examine media use by children and teenagers. The sample consists of 2,032 students from diverse backgrounds via questionnaire, and 694 of these students also completed media diaries. The report analyzes the types of media young people use, the duration of use, with whom they use media, where they use media, media activities they prefer, their home environment, rules that govern media use, and the possible relationship between media use and relations with parents, grades, overall contentedness, and time spent on homework or exercise.

"Zero to Six: Electronic Media in the Lives of Infants, Toddlers and Preschoolers" (2003) used a nationally representative phone survey of 1,000 parents of children age six months to six years about their children's media use, time spent using them, ages they started using each medium, social context for media use, impact on other activities, media environment in the home, parental rules, types of media activities, reading time in relation to other media activities, and the educational attitudes of parents.

Another, smaller survey was conducted in 2003, "Growing Up Wired: Survey on Youth and the Internet in the Silicon Valley," with 804 young people between the ages of ten and seventeen years. Most have basic access to computers and the Internet, with the Internet being used for schoolwork, to communicate with friends, and to a lesser extent to participate in classrooms. Most youth are positive about the use of the Internet in schools. There are some divisions between low and high-income groups along racial lines that are diminished by school access.

Additionally, an issue brief in 2004 examines digital inequality in the United States, moving from a focus on basic access to differences in the quality of access. A brief history of U.S. policy and the digital divide is outlined, with proposals for closing the gap in the quality of access.

All the studies present data about media immersion of infants and teenagers in their everyday lives.

UNESCO

The UNESCO Web site (http://portal.unesco.org) contains a large number of documents. "UNESCO Guidelines for Policy-Making in Secondary School Science and Technology Education" provides a framework for developing policies for older students that has relevance for all educators in specific cultural and educational contexts. It discusses the policy-planning process and provides general goals for science and technology education: scientific literacy in relation to local culture and personal, social, and economic needs; broad and balanced science education throughout schooling to give an appreciation of the processes of scientific research and its relevance for everyday life; measurable progression; ability to revise courses in light of new knowledge and pedagogies; responsiveness to national needs; responsiveness to student needs, skills, and knowledge; technology as a creative process involving hand and mind; and technology involving production and evaluation. There are recommendations for curriculum design, teaching methods, practical work, gender equity, initial teacher training, professional development, language, ICT use, and assessment. The section on ICT includes guidelines for teacher education, and views it as being crucial. It considers adequate ICT technical support staff and maintenance, and pilot studies of innovation in pedagogy using ICT are also important.

Other relevant documents are "UN Literacy Decade: Progress Report 2004–2005," which includes ICT as a central strategy to achieve literacy goals, a paper on developing effective ICT-supported distance education delivery models, and methodologies and development of nonformal education through ICT (a pilot training program). The report "The Place of Science and Technology in School Curricula: A Global Survey of 97 Countries" is also available.

Overall the aims for science and technology education are based on making it locally specific (such as a focus on agriculture in African countries), gender-sensitive, and democratic.

OECD

The Organisation for Economic Co-operation and Development (OECD) Web site (http://www.oecd.org) has numerous resources for ICT and education in general in the Directorate of Education, to be found under the heading "Publications and Documents." There are further resources to be found on related topics, including "Digital Economy and Information Society" and "Information and Communication Technologies." The most significant publication is the report "Learning to Change: ICT in Schools. CERI Project" (2001). It is part of a general project on ICT. Chapter 1 of the document provides reasons to adopt ICT in education that are related to transformed economic and social conditions, the need to acquire new life skills, and the need to extend the range of pedagogies to enhance analytical and higher-order thinking skills. The report explores "quality conditions" that impact on the effective use of ICT. It recommends that there should be radical curriculum change, change to student assessment, digital literacy, adequate resources, quality software, professional training of teachers, school leadership, and links among school, home, and community. The conclusion contains a speech by Seymour Papert on the OECD program launched in 1998 urging governments to understand the radical pedagogical implications of ICT. Findings are clearly stated in point form.

Another set of resources are case studies of educational innovation regarding the use of ICT in specific schools in different OECD countries, such as Australia, Canada, Denmark, Finland, France, Germany, Greece, Japan, Mexico, and the United States. There are two major trends identified. The first represents a shift from rote learning to higher-order skills, in-depth study, problem solving, and collaborative learning. The second is the emphasis on lifelong learning. There are reports on particular schools and a case study synthesis report, "Quo Vademus?—The Transformation of Schooling in a Networked World."

There is also a report titled "Are Students Ready for a Technology-Rich World?" which shows that regular computer users perform better in mathematics tasks and on tests in school contexts. The report also examines computer use at home, attitudes toward computers, and gender inequities.

U.S. Department of Education

The U.S. Department of Education Web site (http://www.ed.gov) has a "Press Room" which includes copies of the speeches associated with various policies from 2001 to the present day and details of government initiatives, the most significant of which is the No Child Left Behind Act (2001). The Office of Educational Technology (OET) is part of the Office of the Secretary of Education. It is responsible for the National Education Technology plan, with an emphasis on strengthening leadership, innovative budgeting for ICT resources, improving teacher training, supporting e-learning and virtual schools, encouraging broadband access, moving toward digital content to replace some textbooks and integrating data systems.

The No Child Left Behind Act of 2001 has core strategies of increased accountability of states, school districts, and schools; greater choice for parents and students; more flexibility for the use of federal funds; and a focus on reading with the aim that every child will be able to read by the end of grade three. Accountability measures involve annual testing based on statewide standards for math and reading in grades three through eight. Students attending schools with poor performances are entitled to transport to a new school. A white paper titled "Meeting the Need for High Quality Teachers: E-Learning Solutions" argues that the quality of teachers is central to achieving positive learning outcomes for students. The paper describes quality requirements and professional development programs. It then goes on to explore various approaches to e-learning professional development programs, with specific case studies and references for further research. The topics include using ICT to facilitate mentoring of teachers, collaboration in the creation of ICT resources, e-learning as a resource for professional development for teachers in distant locations, the creation of professional learning communities, and advantages of self-paced individual learning through online workshops. Another white paper, "How Can Virtual Schools Be a Vibrant Part of Meeting the Choice Provisions of the No Child Left Behind Act" explains the policy of children being able to access funds to go to another school when their own school is underperforming on the tests, and how online learning can provide an alternative. There are examples of online learning schools, and the benefits of online learning and some of the challenges inherent to it are presented. Recommendations are given for states and local authorities on how to set up virtual schools when students only have access to schools that are performing poorly.

Earlier policy documents are also available online. These include "E-Learning: Putting a World Class Education at the Fingertips of All

Children" (2000). This document outlines a government initiative to improve the use of technology for educational purposes. There were five goals established: access to IT in homes, communities, and schools by teachers and students; the effective use of technology to achieve high academic standards; technology and information literacy; research and evaluation of technology use in education; and the development of software and networking to transform teaching and learning. The policy document provides steps for action, success stories and papers on different aspects of the policy. The "Rand Report: Fostering the Use of Educational Technology: Elements of a National Strategy" gives a definition of educational technology and a rationale for its importance in education. There are sections on the current use of technology in schools, examples of best practice, costs of and expenditures on technology in school, and the challenges of providing "technology-enabled schools" such as costs, teacher training, and relevant high-quality software. A basis for a national strategy is then outlined.

Another document, "Getting America's Students Ready for the 21st Century—Meeting the Technology Literacy Challenge: A Report to the Nation on Technology and Education" (1996) gives an overview of the policy hurdles and agenda for using ICT in schools. It defines technological literacy and argues that it should be viewed as an investment for the future. It describes the benefits of technology use for enhanced student achievement. It suggests that technologies can also facilitate an increased role for parents in their child's education and improve teachers' pedagogy. The characteristics of technology-rich schools are highlighted. There is a progress report on meeting technology goals and funding issues, an overview of No Child Left Behind, and a proposal for the role of states, local communities, higher education institutions, and private and nonprofit sectors in promoting technology in education.

"Visions 2020.2: Student Views on Transforming Education and Training Through Advanced Technologies" focuses on the users of new technologies of learning to "highlight market potential" and supplements a prior report that asked experts in the fields of technology and education to imagine the sort of educational practices they envisage for the future. Fifty-five thousand students from across the United States gave "meaningful" responses to an online questionnaire that asked, "What would you like to see invented that you think will help kids learn in the future?" The report explores how K-12 youth use digital technologies, then follows four themes that capture students' visions for the future: digital devices, access to computers and the Internet, intelligent tutors and human helpers, and ways to learn and complete schoolwork using technology.

Apart from these government reports and access to speeches, part of the Web site is devoted to educational technology. It includes resources such as the National Archives Research Catalogue, with photographs, maps, drawings, and manuscripts; Captured Wisdom in Middle School, which shows successful examples of ICT use in classrooms; and Classroom Compass, which has activities and resources to improve teaching of science and mathematics. There are also education consortiums for sharing resources and ideas, professional development, publications, and ideas for leadership. There is an e-learning teacher professional development program that is central to the No Child Left Behind Act (2001) where teachers receive free training in digital workshops and have access to teaching resources and lesson plans.

British Educational Communications and Technology Agency (BECTA).

BECTA is the British agency that was set up to implement and encourage the use of ICT in schools (http://www.becta.org.uk). There are many publications available on the site as well as teaching resources, support services and short discussion papers on topics called *View*. The BECTA document "Supporting Learning and Teaching in Primary Schools: Curriculum Online" specifically addresses educators. It presents the arguments that ICT use in the classroom motivates children to learn, improves learning outcomes, expands pedagogical repertoires, facilitates the sharing and pooling of ideas between teachers, makes some ideas more accessible, and provides new ways for students to conceptualize ideas and to think through problems. British resources for ICT are also listed in this document. There is a discussion of resource and professional development needs, online multimedia resources for lessons that are linked to the curriculum, and exemplary products awards as a way to provide models for other schools. There is a section on Electronic Learning Credits funding for learning resources and a smart guide to develop policies to prioritize the purchase of resources. The role and potential for local authorities are also discussed.

The National Grid for Learning

The National Grid for Learning was an initiative of the British government to facilitate teacher and curriculum professional development and the sharing of ideas about the use of ICT in education. It was first launched at the end of 1997 and is run by BECTA. There is a Virtual Teachers Centre where teachers can exchange ideas about the use of ICT in classrooms. The grid links libraries, universities, community centers, and schools to provide quality-controlled educational resources for schools with selected links to Web sites that can be used by students or teachers. The ICT Excellence Awards for schools, run by BECTA, is a way to give rewards to schools that are successfully integrating ICT in their schools. They can then become an exemplar of good practice from which other schools can gain insights. An example of a resource available on the National Grid for Learning is http://www.waterinschools. com, a site that looks at the history of London's water supply, water conservation, and world water issues and has math exercises based on this theme.

Alliance for Childhood

The Alliance for Childhood promotes hands-on learning, social interaction with caring adults, the importance of play, and relating to nature. Its Web site (http://www.allianceforchildhood.org) has information about the organization, which calls for a moratorium on computers in early and primary school education until comprehensive studies of their effects are conducted. The group argues that technology education should emphasize ethics, responsibility, and critical thinking, and that more advanced technologies should not be introduced until middle school.

A major publication on the Web site is "Fool's Gold: A Critical Look at Computers in Childhood" (2000) This report raises issues such as health and developmental risks, the need for experiences with nature, hands-on creative activities, outdoor play, quality time with caring adults, and time for spontaneous creative play. The authors argue that there should be broad dialogue about computers and children. The organization emphasizes the need for creative, imaginative, ethical, loving, and respectful relationships and play.

A recent publication, "Tech Tonic: Towards a New Literacy of Technology" (2004) has three central arguments: children need a radically different kind of technology education to be able to deal with the ecological crisis confronting humanity; children need more time with nature, caring adults, arts, and hands-on work and play than screen time to develop an ecological ethic; and there is a need to become more active in resisting the high-tech education promoted by government and business because there is evidence that this approach is doing more harm than good. The document proposes a new definition of technology literacy as: "the mature capacity to participate creatively, critically and responsibly in making technological choices that serve democracy, ecological sustainability, and a just society." The report provides ten principles to guide technological literacy and concrete examples of educational programs based on these principles.

NEW CONTEXTS FOR LEARNING

Despite many decades of using ICT in education, there has been a tendency to maintain the same pedagogies and curriculum without taking advantage of the many possibilities for learning offered by ICT. More recently, there have been positive policy initiatives that grapple with the need to change pedagogies and curriculum to equip students for the twenty-first century. There are numerous examples that illustrate how these policy approaches can be put into practice effectively in classroom contexts. Below are resources that consider how to use new technologies for new curriculum with new pedagogies.

Victorian Education Department

There are numerous ICT resources available for teachers and school leaders at the Victorian Education Department's Web site (http://www.sofweb.vic.edu.au/ict). Creating e-Learning Leaders (CeLL) is an initiative that is outlined with support centers and ICT training programs provided across the state. Learning objects are available online to help teachers integrate ICT into their everyday teaching practices. These can be viewed at the Learning Federation (http://www.thelearningfederation.edu.au), which provides ICT resources for specific subject areas. There is an e-learning planning guide that is aimed at school leadership to expand the use of e-learning, providing guidelines for policy making and implementation. The Victorian Education Channel has sites on specific topics created by various organizations that can be used for school projects and building networks between various individuals and organizations. The Knowledge Bank (http://www.sofweb.vic.edu.au/knowledgebank/about.asp) is an online resource that supports the exchange of information about promising practices across the education sector, including some research and examples of ICT use.

South Australian Education Department

The South Australian Education Department Web site has a section on learning technologies and outlines the basic foundations for education from preschool through to year twelve (http://www.decs.sa.gov.au). The Five Essential Learnings go beyond the basics and are designed to equip students as active citizens and learners: futures, identity, interdependence, thinking, and communication. Futures is about perceiving patterns, analyzing challenges for the future, and being

144 • Shift to the Future

able to intervene by building possibilities for preferred futures. Identity includes self-reflection about individual and group identity and developing skills to relate to others. Interdependence involves understanding ethical and practical connections to the world and different cultures and economies, and the need to create sustainable environments. Thinking exposes students to diverse ways of understanding, contrasts different times and cultures to enable reflection on what is valued in the current context, and encourages creativity and the ability to evaluate, plan, and create strategies to develop new ideas. Communication is about understanding the potential application and power of literacy, numeracy, and the use of ICT to communicate, understanding how different forms of communication work, and using a range of types of communication. The curriculum framework is based on a constructivist model of learning that builds on learners' prior knowledge and experience, scaffolds them, and engages them in meaningful learning projects and activities.

A discussion paper titled "Information and Communication Technologies (ICT) in the Early Years" (http://www.earlyyears.sa.edu.au/default.asp?id=7226&navgrp=151) explores how ICT provides opportunities for children to explore, learn, and engage with the world in rich ways. It draws on research already conducted on the effective use of ICT to facilitate children's communication of ideas through media-based design; to play, solve problems, and conduct research; to communicate and share ideas; and to provide links to other children or experts. Examples for using digital cameras, PowerPoint, Web publishing, video production, sound pads, scanners, the Internet, and e-mail are given. New technologies can be compatible with constructive teaching if used appropriately, and can enhance literacy and numeracy goals.

Tasmanian Department of Education

The Tasmanian Department of Education (http://www2education.tas.gov.au) is developing and evaluating policies on the integration of ICT into schools. There is a page that discusses the continuing importance of the provision of resources and investment in ICT, but there has been a shift in emphasis to teacher professional development on new ways of teaching and learning with ICT. A Centre of Excellence in Online Learning has been established to encourage innovative practices and partnership with business.

The key strategies outlined in Learning Together acknowledge the need to reassess what students should know, understand, and value, as well as competencies that need to be developed. It emphasizes technological literacies and engaging students through making the curriculum more relevant to their lives, two significant priorities in an information age.

The document "Department of Education Tasmania: ICT in Education (K-12) Strategic Policy 2002–2005" emphasizes the importance of ICT for improving life chances of students in Tasmanian schools and ways to optimize teaching with ICT. The advantages identified include improving outcomes, student motivation, students working at their own pace, efficiency of administration and assessment, linking to global resources, developing skills for an information age, and enticing investment to Tasmania. The goals are to use ICT to transform pedagogy, curriculum, and organization (from school administration to classroom lessons) to improve student outcomes. The goals are also related to facilitating the development of a community of learners and to equip students with skills for the twenty-first century. In order to achieve these goals there is a need for creative, capable teachers who can use ICT well, ICT support and infrastructure, online resources, sound policies and strategies, and evaluation of best practice. Each of these strategies is outlined in detail in this policy document, including the groups responsible for the implementation of these strategies.

Department of Education and Training, Government of Western Australia

The Curriculum Through ICT program is the core of the Western Australian response to ICT in education (http://www.eddept.wa.edu.au). The program's central principle is that ICT is a learning tool that should be utilized alongside other pedagogical tools and has the potential to expand opportunities for communication, locating information, and performing tasks that have real-world applications. The ICT Innovators section was set up to provide professional development in the effective pedagogical use of ICT in the classroom. It provides the basis for sharing classroom learning activities and for participating teachers to obtain support in development, implementation, and reflection on their teaching practices using technologies. ICT innovators specialize in subject areas and age levels of schooling. The 100 Schools Project has been in operation since 2002 and extends to 2006 as a pilot program, with each school involved having a school-based curriculum ICT coordinator to support teachers, funds for professional development, building learning communities, and infrastructure upgrades. It is planned that the Online Curriculum Systems will have a portal, online teaching and learning system, content management system, and search system.

The latter will regulate the quality and relevance of online resources. Tools to plan, create, communicate, and track online learning activities will also be in place. Another feature of this Web site is the Ideas Bank, which has learning activities related to all the relevant Western Australian learning outcomes. It has specific examples that illustrate how to use ICT in effective ways in classroom practice. There are descriptions of the tasks set, how the classes were conducted, and the technologies used in the process.

Queensland Department of Education

The Queensland Department of Education Web site (http://education. qld.gov.au/corporate/newbasics) outlines the New Basics Project that has three elements: New Basics (what is taught), Rich Tasks (how kids demonstrate that knowledge), and Productive Pedagogies (how it is taught). New Basics is about curriculum reform to address transformations in youth cultures and identities, economy and work, technologies, communities, and cultures. There are trial schools and preliminary research that reflects on the process of reform.

New Basics has a strong emphasis on multiliteracies and communications media, active citizenship facilitated by self-directed learning and team-based projects, and the relationships between environments and technologies. Productive pedagogies promote self-reflection by teachers about what they are teaching, catering to students from diverse backgrounds with different learning styles, and being able to choose teaching strategies that will be most effective in particular contexts. The framework for teaching is productive pedagogies, consisting of four basic priorities: opportunities for students to experiment with ideas, transform meanings, and communicate their work to others; engagement with real-world problems and issues; supporting student-driven inquiry that is challenging and has clear goals and expectations; and encouraging students to value diversity and difference. Rich Assessment Tasks involve integrated knowledge and skills that draw on different disciplines, are intellectually challenging, and involve topics of interest to students yet expand their knowledge of the world. They involve group-based work, focus on identification and solving of real-world issues, and can involve students across classes, year levels, or the whole school in a thematic exploration. The learning is centered on purposive activities with the intention of communicating with an audience and being able to design an approach to research.

International Reading Association

The International Reading Association (http://www.reading.org) is devoted to the dissemination of research to encourage best practices and to improve the quality of reading instruction for all age groups. There is a specialist group within this organization called Technology in Literacy Education. They aim to promote the use of technologies in order to improve the "quality of reading and language arts instruction, and for enhancing children's interest in recreational reading." There are links to publications, including the journals *The Reading Teacher*, *Reading Research Quarterly,* and *Reading Online*. There are many useful articles on the use of ICT for literacy instruction. The International Reading Association also has a position statement titled "Integrating Literacy and Technology in the Curriculum," which is intended to promote dialogue and discussion.

National Council of Teachers of Mathematics

The National Council of Teachers of Mathematics (http://www.nctm.org) promotes mathematics education in the United States through publishing professional journals, professional development, and providing resources to teachers. It has created a set of standards for content, pedagogy, and assessment in math in grades K–12. These are founded on the philosophy and aims of the organization: promoting excellence in math teaching; having qualified teachers with a good foundation in math; developing coherent and complete math curricula; ensuring students develop a good understanding of number, algebra, geometry, measurement, and statistics; emphasizing the central role of teachers; enhancing math thinking and reasoning; applying math to varied contexts and linking math to other subject areas; using calculators and computers; encouraging diverse approaches to problem solving; and evaluating and improving math teaching based on guidance from research.

The NCTM position statement "The Use of Technology in the Learning and Teaching of Mathematics" (http://www.nctm.org/about/position_statements) argues that technologies can help collect, record, organize, and analyze data to extend students' mathematical investigations and understandings. ICT can facilitate higher-order problem solving. The recommendations are to provide adequate resources, support professional development to integrate ICT into math pedagogy, encourage openness to experimentation as part of preservice and in-service professional development, and enable teachers to make informed decisions about when and how to use ICT to teach mathematics.

Colin Lankshear and Michele Knobel

Two literacy educators, Colin Lankshear and Michele Knobel, have a Web site with useful information (http://www.geocities.com/c.lankshear/ourbooks.html). It includes reviews of their books, which have as a common theme the need to transform our understandings about literacy so that we are able to adapt and function in a more complex and technologically saturated society. There are also selected book reviews, a substantial list of references on literacy and technology, and links to the Web sites of other people working in the area. Most useful is the bibliography provided as a basis for further research.

CARET

The Center for Applied Research in Educational Technology provides useful links to Web sites with resources and publications on education and technology (http://caret.iste.org/index.cfm?fuseaction=resources).

MAKING MEANING: TECHNOLOGY AS PLAY

Play is a crucial aspect of the learning process, especially for young children. ICT and "smart toys" can enhance learning if they are appropriate for the age group and used effectively by teachers and parents. Technologies can facilitate play that actively encourages meaning making through storytelling and can enhance learning by moving from the concrete to more abstract understandings. There are many advantages of digital toys and digital software, as additions to other toys in stimulating learning through play. The Web sites below substantiate the educational potential of digital toys and computer software.

DATEC

The DATEC Project (http://www.ioe.ac.uk/cdl/datec/) was a two-year European research initiative that looked at developmentally appropriate technology in early childhood. The aims were to find appropriate uses of ICT to support the development of children in early childhood (up to eight years old) and to provide recommendations and guidance to parents and educators. The research project involved collection of data from the United Kingdom, Sweden, and Portugal in order to gain a cross-cultural perspective on children's interactions and understanding of technologies. The study included programmable toys, video conferencing and closed-circuit TV, software for touch screens, technology and play, collaborative drawing, involving parents, desktop publishing, multimedia authoring, and a wide range of software programs. DATEC also worked to set up experimental school environments in Europe that operated on the basis of clear learning goals, proving their effectiveness, critical comparisons of teaching practices, describing situated learning contexts, evaluations by children of their learning experiences, and examples of children directing their own learning process.

Massachusetts Institute of Technology Media Lab

At the Massachusetts Institute of Technology Media Lab (www.media. mit.edu) there are some projects that relate to toys and play. Cynthia Breazeal and colleagues are developing a huggable interactive teddy bear for children's hospitals and nursing homes that will respond to touch. The aim is to create a toy that responds to being patted, kissed, or tickled. Mitchel Resnick's group, called Lifelong Kindergarten, focuses on education-based projects. Flow Block is an interactive system of light patterns for children to learn about counting, probability, looping, and branching. IDEAS is a network of researchers who discuss ways to use new technologies creatively to enhance educational experiences in after-school centers. Another subgroup is designing programmable Lego bricks for children to learn about engineering and design. There is also another group called Toys of Tomorrow.

David Buckingham

David Buckingham is professor of education at the University of London and the director of the Centre for the Study of Children, Youth and Media. A good place to start a search for articles is at the Literacy Trust: http://www.literacytrust.org.uk/Research/popularreviews. html#Buckingham.

Buckingham is the author of a 2005 literature review, *The Media Literacy of Children and Young People: A Review of the Research Literature* (London: Ofcom), and author or coauthor of other books: *Toys, Games and Media* (coedited with Jeffrey Goldstein, David Buckingham, and Gilles Brouger); *Computer Games: Text, Narrative and Play*; and *Digital Generations: Children, Young People and the New Media*. The review mainly focuses on media literacy with respect to television, radio, the Internet, and mobile telephones. Media literacy is defined as "the ability to access, understand and create communications in a variety of contexts." He draws on studies to argue that sexual predators and financial risks are better addressed through media literacy rather than filtering and blocking. Literature on children's understanding of television, their social and cognitive development, and their media literacy is examined. There is less research on reactions to the Internet, and even less on media such as video and radio. However, there are indications of the possibility for creativity in communication and expression. The review examines factors that impact on the quality and access to media literacy, and this varies for different media. The role of parents, teachers, and government policy is discussed. The report also identifies gaps in the research on this area, such as for specific media, particular groups (i.e., young children), learning progression in media literacy, research based on observations of everyday life, and assessing the effectiveness of media education. This Web site also has useful reviews of a number of other studies in this area.

There is a conference paper titled "The Other Teachers: How Do Children Learn from TV and New Media?" at NESTA Futurelab (http://www.nestafuturelab.org/events/past/bb_pres/db01.htm). Buckingham contends that the new digital divide should not be considered in terms of social class; rather, the difference should be viewed as being between what children are doing inside and outside schools. Media is significant in kids' lives, so in order to make school relevant teachers need to address media and to use ICT in challenging ways. He also uses the example of Pokémon to illustrate the learning potential of games and cards associated with this phenomenon, which is about both commodification and active engagement. It involves game strategy, problem solving and hypotheses, social interactions, and peer tutoring. There is a need for educational games to integrate the learning content with the actual play to make it interesting to kids. He is wary of the idea that learning can be transferred from one context to another, or of idealizing certain activities as "learning communities" when they can be exclusionary. The implications for teaching are that students like to learn together and engage in real, meaningful social practice, and that they need to be in control of their own learning process. We need to be critical of software tools that are often unengaging and the notion that they are all about choice. Finally, Buckingham argues that media education is really about preparing students for dealing with a media-saturated world, and to do this adequately educators need to understand the pleasures associated with media.

At http://www.medienpaed.com there is an article, "Constructing the (Media Competent) Child: Media Literacy and Regulatory Policy in the UK." Buckingham relates the sociological literature that emphasizes children's competencies and autonomy to the idea that children have a media competence, and analyzes British policies in terms of assumptions about childhood. The article focuses on policy debates in Britain about media regulation and children, where there is an increasing emphasis on regulation by the individual. Media literacy is central as a measure to equip children and adults in a media-saturated world. An example is the debate over childhood obesity, where many blame media advertising. Buckingham identifies the complexity of contributing factors. He argues that by the age of eight children are cynical about advertising, yet this does not preclude them being influenced by it. He points to uneasy parallels between corporate media depictions of children as media-savvy and educators' notions of children as media-literate. He also provides two arguments for why self-regulation and the assumption of competence are problematic. Parents are not necessarily able to take on the responsibility for media literacy and regulation, and the state is reneging on its responsibilities. To conclude, Buckingham argues there is a need to move beyond the view of children as media victims or as competent and media-literate, since both are romantic views of the child. There is a need to examine how to develop media literacy, not to assume it already exists.

Televizion Online has an article by Buckingham called "Blurring the Boundaries: 'Teletubbies' and Children's Media Today" at http://www.br-online.de/jugend/izi/english/e-buck.htm. The article discusses the tensions between public/private, education/entertainment, and adult/child dichotomies raised by the debate over the show *Teletubbies*. There is a conflict between the BBC's role as a public broadcaster and the need to remain competitive with children's television. *Teletubbies* fits within a general trend of merchandising associated with TV shows. Critics of the show have argued that it undermines children's language development through baby talk and that there is too little learning of numbers and letters. This debate is situated in the context of the back-to-basics supporters, who are concerned that pleasure, imagination, and play are not about learning. *Teletubbies* is obviously very popular with young children, but it also had youth cult appeal for a short time among teenagers and university students. Buckingham discusses how the responses to children's television by older youth and adults are based on investments in their own childhoods as well as the idea of childhood.

Another longer article is coauthored with Julian Sefton-Green, "Gotta Catch 'Em All: Structure, Agency and Pedagogy in Children's Media Culture." This article uses Pokémon as a case study to explore the relationship between structure and agency without reducing them to an opposition. The authors characterize the Pokémon phenomenon as a cultural practice with distinctive features such as being a two-dimensional puzzle game that leaves much to the children's imagination, caters to different age groups, and appeals to both boys and girls. The game component involves collecting, competing, nurturing, and cooperating. The characters can be very cute or monstrous or both.

They argue not merely that children are consumers of Pokémon but that the different "texts" encourage activity and agency by children, that these games are structured to require knowledge acquisition, that children are able to apply knowledge, and that they interact socially whilst playing with Pokémon. The article then discusses debates around pedagogy and their relevance for understanding Pokémon in terms of consumer training or development of cognitive and social skills, and creating learning communities.

CACHET Study

The CACHET study (http://www.ioe.stir.ac.uk/CACHET/research. htm) looks at the different types of interactions children have with "smart toys" and associated software in the informal and formal contexts of home, primary school, and out-of-school groups. The research draws on video analysis, interviews, diaries, and a sticker rating system. The data collection is based on the Wechsler Preschool and Primary Scale of Intelligence—Revised (WPPSI-R) and the Preschool Play Behaviour Scale (PPBS) to rank verbal and nonverbal abilities for age-appropriate levels. The types of interactions are coded in terms of action/gesture, expression/gaze, and dialogue, which can be between children; between the toy and children; between the toy, computer software characters, and children; or between the child and researcher. The toys have a vocabulary of about four thousand words and respond to the child squeezing their ears or hands. The toys act as helpers when the children use the software, or alternatively there is an online help function with a 2-D version of the soft toy. Many children chose to keep the toy turned off and preferred adult help rather than to receive help from the toy. However, the toy in combination with the software significantly increased social interactions between children. While these particular toys weren't very good at providing useful help, tangible interfaces such as soft toys have a lot of potential to address the emotional as well as cognitive needs of children when they are learning. They also may redress the gender imbalance by making computers more approachable and enhance access to students with less advanced verbal and nonverbal skills. Additionally, they do not make any difference to children's imaginative play. An article by Luckin et al., "Children's Interactions with Interactive Toy Technology," draws similar conclusions that "smart toys" can address the "affective and the effective dimensions of learners' interactions" to make learning fun and accessible, and that children can traverse different interfaces readily. It also discusses these toys in the context of educational theories about scaffolding, the need for graded help interventions to support learners, and the importance of peer discussion to learn. This suggests development of interactive toy technology needs to understand how help should be made available to small children. "Out of the Box, but in the Zone? Can Digital Toy Technology Provide a More Able Peer for Young Learners?" explores the study on interactive toys again. It looks in more detail at the extent to which children use the toy's help function when working through the software.

Plowman and Stephen provide a literature review of the use of ICT by young children in formal and informal contexts called "A Benign Addition? Research on ICT and Pre-school Children." They point to how the literature indicates that ICT has not transformed teaching practices and is often narrowly focused on desktop computers. They then discuss the debate over the value and use of ICT with young children, referring to government policies and contributions from researchers or organizations. The issues raised are whether or not children are passive or active when they use ICT, problems of commodification and exploitation of children, pornography and violence, parental attitudes toward the Internet, the link between violent content and aggressive behavior, the physical effects of using ICT, and the impact on brain/cognitive development. The last concern may be sidestepped by the development of tangible ICT objects as manipulatives for developing skills in the early years. They argue the issue should not be whether or not to use computers, but how to use technology with children to effectively enhance learning. The review then goes on to discuss studies of media use and how a demarcation between entertainment and education, or between learning and play, has been undermined. Notions of literacy have been adapted to accommodate the needs of a knowledge economy. There are studies on how ICT can be used for language development, the importance of visual literacy, the ability to navigate screens on the computer, and diverse contexts and media for communication. Navigating diverse texts is crucial. Other issues are that hardware is not designed for young children, though there are more interactive electronic toys available for creative and collaborative play. Research projects on various interactive toys and software are discussed. The Internet is still inaccessible to young children because of the extensive text, but CD-ROMs can be suitable. There are also problems with actually identifying what software will work for young children. The review includes a critical analysis of the Web sites that can be used by parents and educators for guidance about software and toys.

"Between the Lines: Documenting the Multiple Dimensions of Computer-Supported Collaborations" examines three case studies, including the interactive toys, to investigate collaborative learning situations. Ecolab is a software environment for children age nine through eleven to build a mini world of plants and animals, to provide a simulated environment, and to explore the relationships between organisms through a series of activities. Children can get help at different levels of assistance. The Galapagos CD-ROM has sections on Darwin's visit to the islands and his theory of evolution. Students use an online notepad to explain the variations in life on the islands. They can view one possible answer after they write fifty words on the notepad. The research framework for all these case studies is to document the type of interactions between the child and computer (and/or toy), and the extent of collaboration between students.

Commercial Toy Sites: Children's Technology Review

The Children's Technology Review has reviews of children's software and technology products (http://www.childrenssoftware.com). Fisher-Price toys has a range of smart toys for young children and babies (http://www.fisher-price.com). LeapFrog is another source of educational toys (http://www.leapfrog.com). Play School (http://www.abc.net.au/children/play), Teletubbies (http://www.bbc.co.uk/cbeebies/teletubbies), and Sesame Street (http://pbskids.org/sesame) are sites with games and resources for young children.

THINKING AND KNOWING: INFORMAL LEARNING AT HOME AND IN COMMUNITIES

There are advantages of out-of-school contexts that demonstrate the potential to enhance learning through ICT. Educators can draw on some of the features of these environments and their successes to facilitate more effective use of ICT in school classrooms. After-school computer clubhouses show that play, peer social interaction, self-directed activities, individually paced learning, adult or expert support, and varied activities are conducive to positive learning environments. Lessons derived from an examination of games culture can be applied to formal educational contexts.

Computer Clubhouse

The Computer Clubhouse Web site (http://www.computerclubhouse.org) aims to promote a clubhouse learning approach and supports ninety Computer Clubhouses across the world that cater to disadvantaged communities. The aim is to create spaces in which youth can develop their ICT skills, become confident in using computers, and explore their own ideas in a supportive environment. The *Computer Clubhouse Quarterly Newsletter* has articles about the centers and is accessible at this Web site.

Fifth Dimension

The virtual Fifth Dimension (http://129.171.53.1/blantonw/5dClhse/clearinghl.html) is a collective of literacy after-school enrichment programs across the United States, Mexico, Australia, and Russia that are multigenerational learning environments with an emphasis on interactive technologies. It is a play world/make-believe activity system that is educational. Diversity of language and literacies is the goal, with play being central to the learning process. Fifth Dimension activities include playing computer and board games, drawing, reading stories, communication with children at other sites, multimedia, and group and individual work. Young participants are assisted by high school and university students and adult volunteers. Fifth Dimension research has shown that students who participate in Fifth Dimension, including special education students, achieve higher results on reading and math achievement tests.

In the Fifth Dimension there are mythical characters such as 'The Entity" and "The Wizard," who can assist the children navigate their way through the various sites, and act as mediators. The Fifth Dimension site has a maze with twenty rooms, each with two or more kinds of activities linked to subjects across the curriculum. Usually the activities involve some type of problem solving and higher-order thinking. Tasks need to be performed by participants before they can move to another game. Examples of such tasks are writing to others, making a video, or creating an art work. A journey log captures each child's learning process. Children make choices about their path through their maze and between activities in the rooms, and they are encouraged to set their own goals. The activities are meaningful and purposive while teaching basic skills. They involve a lot of self-direction with adults as co-participants alongside children. There are many opportunities for authentic problem solving, group collaboration, and communication about the process and end result. It is a collaborative learning environment that encourages communication.

Screenplay Project

A paper based on the Screenplay project by Ben Williamson and Keri Facer, "More than 'Just a Game': The Implications for Schools of Children's Computer Games Communities" is available at NESTA Futurelab (http://www.nestafuturelab.org/research/draft/02draft02.htm). The paper discusses peer group dynamics in game playing among peers, techno-culture that provides resources for game playing, and the ways games have Web sites or dynamics within the games that encourage learning on how to play and how these might be transferred to classroom learning. The paper draws on interviews from the Screenplay project to illustrate key points. Social dynamics included children taking on roles of teachers and learners, the sharing of resources, different levels of participation, discussions about games, competition, evaluation of games, and status according to ability such as "expert gamers." Techno-culture magazines, Web site forums and official guides can give some children "cultural capital" in working out strategy and what are the best new games. Many games are also linked to media culture through film. Some games are very complex and involve learning communities where players can form teams and share information about how to play effectively. Applying knowledge of game playing to education requires an appreciation of the social practices surrounding gaming and providing challenging tasks for children, rather than merely looking at games in terms of interfaces. Additionally, meaning making is part of the game, and games involve multimodality. The lesson that can be derived from games is that education should involve "authentic practices" and should provide support networks from peers and experts, and teaching children how to use tools and resources for self-directed and group-based learning.

NEW WAYS OF LEARNING IN SCHOOL

The previous sections have addressed innovative approaches to curriculum, pedagogies, and learning environments. There is also the need to reconceptualize the foundational skills of numeracy and literacy for the information age. The resources below examine how to move beyond the basics to higher-order skills. Multiliteracies accommodate diverse learning styles and different ways to acquire knowledge and represent the learning process. Mathematics knowledge can be applied and linked to everyday activities. Multimedia and ICT are learning tools that expand learning opportunities and skills.

Learning by Design

Learning by Design (http://www.l-by-d.com) is a Web site that provides tools and resources for teachers to reflect on their pedagogy and share classroom lessons. The Web site has the background to the project and a page on multiliteracies, outlines Learning by Design principles, provides resources and research projects, and has examples of classroom practice shared by other teachers. Learning by Design is a collaborative project between Royal Melbourne Institute of Technology (RMIT) and Common Ground Publishing and teachers in Australia and Malaysia. It is a practical basis for teachers' professional development. Learning elements facilitate planning, documenting, and sharing of teacher resources.

The Learning by Design principles are engagement with learner diversity; multiliteracies and meaning making; teaching as a reflective planned process; how learning should cater to the need for belonging as well as transformation; and how teaching can be understood through knowledge processes.

Respect for learner diversity is not just about group identities based on age, ethnicity, language, gender, sexual orientation, socioeconomic group, and locale; it is also about individual life experiences, values, sensibilities, learning styles, and affinities. Thus teaching needs to involve flexible delivery, support varied knowledge processes, and cater to different student interests. However, while teachers need to draw on the interests and orientations of their students, they should also extend them beyond what is known to expand their horizons. Multiliteracies involves different modes of communication—linguistic, visual, audio, gestural, and spatial. This does require teachers to extend their own literacies and pedagogical repertoires. Knowledge processes are central to being reflexive about teaching practice in order to vary the forms of knowledge acquired. They are based on experiencing the known or the new, applying knowledge in appropriate ways or creatively, conceptualizing by naming or with theory, and analyzing functionally or critically. Through stepping back from the teaching process, teachers can work out whether they emphasize certain types of knowledge processes at the expense of others, in order to expand and experiment with their classroom planning.

Learning by Design facilitates planning, documenting, and sharing at three levels: Learning Elements focus on classroom lessons for a single topic, Learning Frameworks focus on documenting curriculum across a number of Learning Elements, and Learning Communities document the programs and organization of a community of learning.

There are references on this Web site to the works by the New London Group on multiliteracies, which provide the theoretical basis for this project. Research projects that are related to multiliteracies and Learning by Design are also outlined.

New London Group

Education Australia Online explains the background to the New London Group and lists the participants who met in New London, New Hampshire, for five days in September 1994 (http://edoz.com.au/educationaustralia/archive/features/mult3.html). From this session came a jointly authored paper, "A Pedagogy of Multiliteracies: Designing Social Futures." This initial research has created offshoots in research projects around the world that take the research in new directions. The article can be found online at http://wwwstatic.kern.org/filer/blog-Write44ManilaWebsite/paul/articles/A_Pedagogy_of_Multiliteracies_Designing_Social_Futures.htm.

The article argues that there is a need for a different approach to literacy pedagogies that the New London Group names multiliteracies. Changes to the social environment necessitate a rethinking of literacy to encompass diverse modes of communication and media forms, and an increasing cultural and linguistic diversity. Being able to navigate through this complex new reality of work and community requires a broader conception of literacy. The article also describes the processes of discussion and how the concept of multiliteracies evolved. Local and global connectedness and diverse modes of meaning making including the spatial, visual, audio, behavioral, and kinesthetic involve new literacies. The article then goes on to describe changes to work, citizenship, and lifeworlds that place different demands on the education system. "Designs for meaning" is the term used because it can be about the end product or the process. Designs are either already available, can involve the active process of designing, or can be redesigned and adapted. This theoretical approach assumes that learning occurs through embodied, situated, and social contexts. Bearing this in mind, teachers can categorize their pedagogy in terms of situated practice, overt instruction, critical framing, and transformed practice.

Abstracts and some full-text versions of articles on multiliteracies are available on the Web site Activated (http://activated.det.act.gov.au/reading/curr_jour-hotlists-multiliteracies.htm). A paper by Gunther Kress on multimodality is available (http://www.ched.uct.ac.za/literacy/papers/KressPaper.html). And NESTA Futurelab has a simple introduction to the concepts of multimodality, multisemiotics, and multiliteracies (http://www.nestafuturelab.org/viewpoint/art49.htm).

Multimodality is a term that captures the multiple modes of communication based on the senses of sight, hearing, touch, smell, and taste. Multisemiotics links meanings that can be generated from different modes and the ways our interpretation of meanings are based on a particular life history and experiences and cultural background. There are potentially multiple interpretations of any given communication. Multiliteracies is about understanding diverse forms of media and modes of communication, and being able to produce diverse types of texts.

Douglas Clements

Professor Douglas Clements is an associate dean for educational technology at the State University of New York at Buffalo's Graduate School of Education who has published extensively in the areas of math education, educational technology, and early childhood education. Many of his articles and research projects can be accessed on his Web site (http://www.gse.buffalo.edu/faculty/viewfaculty.asp?id=7), including the research project "Building Blocks: Foundations for Mathematical Thinking, Pre-Kindergarten to Grade 2: Research-Based Materials Development." The materials can be found at http://www.gse.buffalo.edu/org/buildingblocks/about.htm. The articles examine the research process for building blocks, analyze the problems with current mathematical software, outline the pedagogical basis for children's learning of basic math, provide examples of exercises for students that enhance math learning, and explore the idea that young children should only use concrete manipulatives. There is a general emphasis on the need to understand the development needs of children and how they actually learn and to systematically test the software.

Building Blocks is a series of mathematics curriculum materials that use print, manipulatives, and computers. The underlying philosophy is that math activities need to be linked to children's everyday activities. For instance, children like puzzles, so these are used to engage children with basic geometry principles; also, children are more likely to learn about numbers if counting or sequences involve real-world scenarios. The focus on spatial and geometric competencies and numeric and quantitative skills involves three other aspects of foundational math skills. These are patterns and functions, data, classifying, sorting, and sequencing.

The article "Building Blocks for Young Children's Mathematical Development" outlines the seven-step design process for the development of Building Blocks. The first part of the article provides a rationale for the research project based in the inadequacies of math software and the lack of empirical and theoretical support to develop and assess them. The first stage of the research was to identify what should be taught. This was based on educational research into what children understand about math—choosing to zoom in on geometry and shapes and numeric and quantitative concepts. After this, the researchers observed students and conducted interviews to delineate the variation in the ability of students to compose and decompose shapes. The next phase involved creating a basic design for the software that was based on children's activities and knowledge of cognitive processes. The notion of concrete versus on-screen manipulatives is discussed. Then the research tested the software using interviews and observations of a small number of children to try to understand how children interpret, act, and respond in order to refine the resources. Phase five involved making the activities more attuned with children's everyday activities, such as setting a table and making cookies involving counting and quantities. Then the materials were tested in a classroom setting. The concluding phase is to make the research and software available in classrooms.

Apollo Parkways Primary School Projects

Apollo Parkways Primary School has a Web site (http://web.apollo-parkps.vic.edu.au) that showcases school projects focusing on themes such as Discovering Democracy, Science Week, Italian Week, Water Quality, Global Crime Scene Investigation, and Environmental Education. One example is Landscaping Designs, which involved third and fourth graders mapping the garden beds they had designed and planted during Arbor Week. This exercise involved measuring to scale and using compasses. There is also a habitat program as part of environmental education that is about educating the school and broader local community to create habitats for fauna through planting indigenous species. Global Crime Scene Investigation involves schools being given a case with suspects at the school. Students then collect evidence and work out who is the prime suspect. This is discussed using Ichat/AOL; video footage of the arrest is put on the Web site.

Investigations in Number, Data, and Space

Investigations is a K-5 curriculum design to teach mathematics (http://investigations.scottforesman.com/overview.html). The curriculum is organized into units of three to eight weeks on different topics. The activities encourage creativity, collaboration, and higher-order thinking, and students are asked to justify and explain their thinking. They aim to address the diversity of learning styles of students and to build knowledge systematically. There are suggestions about children's literature that can be utilized to teach mathematics. Computers are integrated into the curriculum to enable students to understand and visualize mathematics in different ways to reinforce mathematical concepts.

There are also tools for ongoing assessment to track students' progress individually and as a whole class. The Web site advertises professional development packages, videotapes, and resource books for teaching mathematics. There are sheets that explain investigations to families and teachers. Letters to Families explain each new unit to parents, how it is relevant to everyday life, and what work can be done at home to expand on the learning in the classroom. There is a sheet on how games are an engaging way of teaching math at school and at home. Some sample activities are also available on this Web site.

NEW LEARNING IN THE THIRD MILLENNIUM

Innovation and creativity should be at the center of the learning experiences in schools in the third millennium. The resources below provide examples of models for schooling that maximize the potential for creativity, applying knowledge, and learning how to learn. Researchers advocate the need to re-create schools as spaces for collaborative learning and reconceptualize schools as knowledge-building communities. Alternative schools such as Reggio Emilia, Montessori, and Rudolf Steiner are examples of school philosophies, pedagogies, and environments that emphasize creativity and child-centered learning. New technologies provide an opportunity to rethink pedagogy and curriculum. They affirm a recurrent theme: the need to reform schools so authentic learning and knowing how to learn are emphasized.

Massachusetts Institute of Technology Media Lab

The Massachusetts Institute of Technology Media Lab (www.media. mit.edu) is a research laboratory with a degree program that was founded by Nicholas Negroponte in 1985 as a space to bring together disciplines in a focus on digital innovation. The diversity of research includes creating new software, researching how children learn, and exploring the technologies of human and machines, speech interfaces, interface design, interactive cinema, object-oriented video, nanomedia, and spatial imaging.

There are research groups set up with each Media Lab faculty member. Of particular relevance is the group The Future of Learning, run by David Cavallo and Seymour Papert, which addresses the gap between rhetoric on the need to change education for the twenty-first century and organizational/curriculum/pedagogical constraints from education systems suited to the industrial age. The approach taken by the research group has a critical component that emphasizes understanding and changing ways of thinking that limit educational potentials from the integration of ICT. Another aspect is to create a conceptual framework to argue for more holistic approaches to digital-based learning. Finally, the activist element aims at change at an individual and small-group level, as well as on a national and international level. In 2006 the stated goal is to develop an international network of innovative examples of ICT in education, called the Learning Hub, in order to use the project's success as a basis to promote new ideas generally.

Research group projects that stem from this research group include Constructionism, Content for the Digital Age, GoGo Board, Learn to Teach: Learn to Learn, Learning and Community Development, Mega-Change in Learning, RoBallet, The City That We Want, Learning with a Hundred-Dollar Computer, and Speaking on the Record. All of these groups have an educational/ICT focus. Links are on the Media Lab Web site.

UltraLab

The UltraLab has numerous research projects, media articles, and papers available on the Web site (http://www.ultralab.anglia.ac.uk). UltraLab is a "learning technology centre at Anglia Polytechnic University" that conducts research on the benefits of new technologies as learning environments. One research initiative is Learning in the New Millennium, which is about building a learning community of school students, teachers, and scientists and engineers from Nortel. The TESCO School Net 2000 is another venture that involves setting up a Web site for children, by children, with teachers in an advisory role. CarnaudMetalBox schools is a Web site that provides links to other educational Web sites as a teacher resource for utilizing online searches for student research or online learning activities. UltraLab has cocreated learning community tools for children with Oracle and has created TeacherNet in the UK to promote the use of ICT and to support teachers' professional development.

There are also a collection of papers on the site. These include "Computers Don't Bite" (1998). This article supports teachers' professionalism and carefully argues for how ICT can enhance teaching practice through providing unique opportunities for contacts with scientists and people from different cultures, modeling of hypotheses, the exchange and drafting of writing, and experimentation with visual art and design. The main emphasis is on the importance of the role of the teacher; the premise is that "the computer is not a teaching machine, it is a learning tool." ICT provides a context for teachers to reflect on their pedagogy.

The article "Student Revolution" describes the rapid pace of technological change, research that shows how kids can do exceptional and creative things with computers, and the British policy program including the National Grid for Learning (which is a communication center about good pedagogical practice using new technologies), and argues that not all software is positive for learning outcomes, such as the "drill and kill" activities.

The article "Teachers, Teaching and Technology in the New Millennium" (1999) posits two options for pedagogical approaches to ICT use: technical mastery with rote learning approaches or teachers as action researchers who explore new ways to engage and stimulate students using technologies.

The "ETUI Public Report" is about experimental school environments set up with the support of Pomeu Fabra, Apple Computer, and UltraLab. Focus families in Spain, Norway, and the United Kingdom are participants in the study, which aims to create a toy that can learn and be taught on the basis of research with a number of elements: software development and test environment, a taxonomy of software and artifacts, familiarizing children with different screen environments, hardware development, older children reflecting on their earlier learning experiences, observations of children playing with toys at home, utilizing online communities, trialing toys, and children communicating about them online.

UltraLab was also a major contributor to an independent report on the use of ICT in British schools called "The Stevenson Report: The ICT in UK Schools Report" that has two key recommendations: there is a need to improve ICT hardware, software, and teacher professional development, and government must prioritize the use of ICT in schools by providing adequate resources, leadership, and professional development.

NESTA Futurelab

This Web site is an excellent resource for publications on the impact of technology on learning and teaching (http://www.nestafuturelab. org) There are research reports, workshops, innovation reports, papers, online journals, book reviews, literature reviews, handbooks, and discussion papers. Futurelab brings together creative and technology communities with educators in order to think about how to enrich learning environments with technology.

The literature reviews cover diverse topics such as learning with tangible technologies, e-assessment, games and learning, science education and ICT, creativity, technology and learning, thinking skills and ICT, mobile technologies and learning, digital technologies in museums, science centers and galleries, informal learning with technology outside school, primary science and ICT, citizenship, technology and learning, and languages, technologies, and learning. The literature review "14-19 and Digital Technologies: A Review of Research and Projects" focuses on core issues such as the purpose of education, who should benefit, and what sort of citizens, workers, and learners we want to produce. They then explore how these debates can frame our understanding of the use of technologies for learning in terms of conventional teaching practices or a transformation of pedagogy. The literature review on primary science and ICT looks at the role of teachers and learners, knowledge of the subject area, the need to balance learning about scientific information and learning to do science, and assessment. It critically evaluates the use of ICT in primary science teaching.

The Futurelab handbooks explore the role that digital technologies may play in education in the future by drawing on the perspectives of teachers, researchers, and children. One such project is Games and Learning, which examines the latest educational games and whether schooling should be altered to integrate these games into classroom teaching. Another handbook addresses the need to transform education to encourage creative and collaborative learning in order to function in the knowledge society. The "Designing Educational Technologies with Users" handbook advises on ways that educators and developers of digital educational resources could work together to make more relevant, age-appropriate, and intellectually challenging educational software. The "Personalisation and Digital Technologies" report has an underpinning premise that education should conform to learners' needs rather than the other way round. ICT can facilitate this approach by allowing learners to make informed choices and direct their own learning, drawing on and recognizing diverse skills and knowledge, creating diverse contexts for learning, and developing assessment tasks that help the learner to learn.

Marlene Scardamalia and Carl Bereiter

An article by Marlene Scardamalia and Carl Bereiter, "Computer Support for Knowledge-Building Communities" (http://carbon.cudenver.edu/~bwilson/building.html), explores how the use of an enabling technology such as computer-supported intentional learning environments (CSILEs) can transform schools into knowledge-building communities. They discuss how schools should be modeled like sciences, where there is collaborative learning and continuous adaptation to new contributions to knowledge. The emphasis is on the development of expertise that is defined as "a process of progressive problem solving and advancement beyond present limits of competence." Unfortunately, schools focus on individuals at the expense of collaborative and communal projects, emphasize formal and quantifiable knowledge rather than knowledge that can be related to practical problems, tend not to make knowledge objectives known to students, and do not develop students' expertise over time. Alternatively, Scardamalia and Bereiter argue for peer review and creating collective knowledge, recognition from peers, communication of project results to broader audiences, longer-term projects, engagement with others in the school and outside the school, open-ended projects that build on students' questions and interests, and access to various data. CSILEs facilitate this approach through making students' work accessible to other students through a database, where students can make commentaries, raise questions, and justify links to new activities. The information flow can be multidirectional and asynchronous, encourage questions, facilitate multimodal expressions of ideas, allow time to reflect on ideas, and show the cumulative basis of research. Teachers have found that students perform beyond their usual capabilities in this learning context.

NAACE Report

The National Advisory Committee on Creative and Cultural Education report "All Our Futures: Creativity, Culture and Education" is available at http://www.artscampaign.org.uk/campaigns/education/summary.html. The report's central argument is that creative and cultural education is central for meeting economic and social needs in the twenty-first century. Creative education is defined as education that develops "young people's capacities for original ideas and education," while cultural education enables students to deal with diversity and complexity in the social realm. The report presents a case for an emphasis on creativity, what needs to be done, current educational practices, obstacles and opportunities for implementing reform, and a national strategy. The themes of the report are that there are significant challenges due to changes in economy and society that require a new agenda in education; creativity is involved in all disciplines and areas of human activity; creativity involves a balance among knowledge, skills, and innovation; young people need to be adaptable to rapid cultural change; and creative and cultural education should be integrated across the curriculum. The first part of the report sets out the framework for creative and cultural education, as well as a rationale for this reform agenda. The second section of the report looks at the significance of such a shift for curriculum, pedagogy, and assessment. Part three considers the need for partnerships between schools and other groups, and for resources and professional development. The last section of the report has detailed policy recommendations for a national strategy.

The Learning Federation (TLF)

The Learning Federation produces online curriculum content for teachers in Australia and New Zealand and was set up by state, territory, and national governments. Examples of interactive multimedia learning objects and digital resources are described and provided on their Web site, together with documents that describe the rationale and support their use (http://www.thelearningfederation.edu.au/tlf2/default_ori.asp). For example, in the curriculum area "Innovation, Enterprise and Creativity," the Web site states that by using the resources, "students are compelled to explore, take risks, analyse and synthesise information, think critically, solve problems and make decisions." In addition to the learning objects, there are digital resources that include moving images, images of documents, paintings, maps, photographs, songs, and broadcasts. They are sourced from institutions such as national archives, museums, private collections, and art galleries. These have much more potential to be appropriated by students in innovative ways for knowledge building than learning objects that characteristically reproduce textbook examples on screens and do not generally extend opportunities for new learning

Reggio Emilia

The Clearinghouse on Early Education and Parenting Web site (http://ceep.crc.uiuc.edu/poptopics/reggio.html) has a section on the Reggio Emilia approach that includes an electronic discussion list, publications, videos, bibliography, and links to Web sites and Web articles about this form of early childhood education. There are also two Web sites with resources such as articles, books, and videos on the Reggio Emilia approach (http://www.mpi.wayne.edu/reggioresources.htm and http://members.aol.com/ouidameier/reggio/cavallo_bib.htm).

A Reggio Emilia school was set up in the town of that name in Italy forty years ago, and networks of these schools were created in the 1970s. The schools emphasize the resourcefulness, curiosity, and communicative capacities of children, projects rather than a set curriculum linked to a time frame, relationships with the community, a studio for creative expression, and child-centered learning. They encourage intercultural dialogue and experiences linked to the environment. There is a strong emphasis on multisensory learning. The aesthetic environment includes a piazza in the center of the school where children, parents, and teachers can gather to meet and do various activities. Learning spaces include objects usually associated with home and are not simple designs premised on children liking only bright, simple objects. This democratic approach to education arose in reaction to fascism and the need to rebuild Italy's economy and civil society.

A useful Web site is that of Project Approach based on Reggio Emilia principles (http://www.project-approach.com/foundation/teaching.htm). It provides detailed ways to plan lessons for different age groups around real-world topics and projects, with actual projects that have been carried out in classrooms. Projects are in-depth investigations of real-world topics that can be carried out by a class or small groups of children, and are structured to cross over disciplines and skills and to engage students in challenging tasks. For young children it is believed that play encourages children to explore materials, ideas, and relationships, while systematic instruction facilitates the acquisition of skills by older children. Project work builds on these skills through learning how and when to apply them in real-world situations. Project work links to the curriculum, but it is planned in negotiation with the children and relates to their own stated interests. The advantages of projects are that they can allow children many ways of exploring, understanding, and representing the topic under investigation. They can involve mastery of symbol systems as well as hands-on manipulative experience. Learning that revolves around a class project involves more cooperation and memorable experiences, and children get a sense of why they are learning skills from different subject areas.

There are criteria for selecting project topics based on whether the topic is interesting for the children; is a real-world topic; draws on first-hand experience from fieldwork; encourages children to develop their own questions, then to draw on adults' (including expects) knowledge of a topic area (if needed); allows scope for children to ask questions and investigate them; facilitates children learning in myriad ways; enables children to apply mathematical, scientific, artistic, imaginative, dramatic, and literary skills; and can relate to a new project. The stages of planning include an event to stimulate the interest of the class; children mapping out their current understandings of the topic and listing questions; and preparation for fieldwork so that students children know what questions they want to address, how they will record what they observe, and what they want to bring back to the classroom. After the fieldwork the children discuss and represent what they have learned, and consolidate their knowledge through research and further questions. To conclude the project there is a final event for children to share their knowledge with others, and they are encouraged to be selective about what they want to include in their presentation. Finally, the class reflects on their learning experiences through creative activities such as writing stories, creating artwork, doing a play, making a film, or writing a song.

An example of such a project was one that had water as its focus. The idea grew out of another project on rocks when children noticed condensation in the rock garden. This U.S. primary school was located near the banks of the Illinois River, providing a local context to explore the topic. Parents were sent a letter to inform them about the project. The teacher told personal stories about water, then asked the children to think about events in their lives that involve water. They discussed these, then illustrated them with various materials and wrote brief descriptions of their stories. The children then grouped their pictures and labeled them to display them in the hall. Then the class was asked questions about water, such as: How is it measured? What is it made of? Where does it come from and where can you find it? What can it do and what is it used for? The children were encouraged to share, think, and write about these issues and write their own question. A field trip involved going to the Grafton Water Works to look at the water filtration system and pipes to the river, having lunch at a restaurant with a huge fish tank, and going down to the river to measure the temperature and do sketches. An environmental educator also came to the class to discuss issues with them. The children predicted the amount of drinking water that comes from different sources on the earth. The educator also discussed the wetlands and used a sponge to show how wetlands soak up water and a coffee filter to demonstrate that rivers act as filtration systems. A visit to wetlands reinforced this knowledge when a park ranger taught children a game that showed the importance of the wetlands for wildlife. Again the children took field notes and did drawings. From these information resources children estimated and measured the volume of water, measured the temperature of water, observed what objects sink or float, made Venn diagrams comparing water samples, and used water drops as magnifiers. They created posters with information and brought in water samples from different sources. During the project children wrote stories in their daily journals and kept writing questions. Individual and groups of children engaged in different tasks that they set themselves. For instance, two children made a salt relief map of the states on the border of the Mississippi River, two other children built a model of the water department building, a group made a mountain with a running waterfall, a group sketched and made boats, two students interviewed students in the school, one student investigated what would dissolve in water, another set up an experiment to see what chemicals were in water, other students made papier-mâché models of fish and turtles, and another student made a water game. Finally children invited various guests to a presentation that included a movie with narrated drawings on a roll of paper and a percussion performance to re-create a thunderstorm, and each child showed a guest the work displayed in the room.

A simpler, shorter project in another class arose from the spontaneous interest of two children in working out why and at what rate puddles disappear. They drew chalk lines around the puddles, measuring the distance across, and measuring them every half hour after this. Such an exercise involved mathematical skills of measurement and subtraction and scientific concepts based on investigating an everyday experience. They were asked to predict, observe, measure, record, discuss, hypothesize, reason, and explain, as well as to present to other students their findings and how they had carried out their study. They had already gained skills in math and science and were applying them in this context. Other children investigated what materials let water through and which ones were waterproof. Three children created a store that sold goods for wet weather. This involved using a cash register and sorting, grouping, and counting store items. Other children read books about the weather, water, and plumbing. A number of children drew and observed an umbrella; a number of their drawings required some mathematical knowledge of angles and measurement and an understanding of how the folding mechanism worked.

Another useful source is the Reggio Children document at http://zerosei.commune.re.it/pdfs/foldrerch/RCH-ENGLISH.pdf. This international center was established to defend and promote the rights and potential of all children by respecting each child's identity, individuality, and competence. They believe that education should involve active, constructive, and creative learning. The organization values research on childhood and the documenting and sharing of children's and teachers' work using multimedia. They promote the idea that research is an attitude that involves openness to new possibilities in a changing world and is as important for children as adults. There is an emphasis on teaching values of respect, intercultural education, environmental awareness, and social justice. The organization facilitates global connections between teachers, researchers, and nongovernmental organizations. Reggio Children manages an exhibition, "The Hundred Languages of Children," that demonstrates children's creativity and learning through projects in preschools and primary schools.

Montessori Schools

The International Montessori Index (http://www.montessori.edu) has information on the Montessori method, Montessori schools, Montessori environments, and materials and related resources. Montessori education emphasizes creativity, problem solving, social and time management skills, and children contributing to society and the environment. The emphasis is on individual choice of research and projects, not on being given major time constraints by adults. It aims to foster a learning environment for children to reach their spiritual, emotional, physical, and intellectual potential, yet encourages children to view themselves as members of local communities, global citizens, and earth stewards. Children are learning how to learn, and classrooms are organized as mixed-age groups. Montessori education was founded in 1907 by an Italian physician, Dr. Maria Montessori.

Montessori is distinguished from traditional education by the fact that the children are encouraged to use all five senses for their learning and learn at their own pace and according to their own choice among diverse possibilities. In the Montessori approach to learning there is a recognition that it involves self-discipline by students, community-based learning, and older children helping younger children. There are work centers for various subjects, and children choose what subjects they will spend time on. There are no grades. Assessment is by portfolio and teachers' observations. Children are given character education such as life skills, etiquette, and doing community work.

For children from birth to age six the emphasis is on contact with the environment, movement, being in tune with all the senses, establishing respect and self-respect, and developing an appreciation of beauty. From ages six to twelve, children produce charts, models, books, timelines, maps, books, and plays, and the environment is kept simple so that children can be creative. The Web site http://www.michaellolaf.net provides an overview of Montessori philosophy, including specifics of teaching children at certain age levels. For instance, there is a series of puzzles described that stimulate children ages one to three years to become interested in colors and shapes, to use different muscles, to handle materials, and to problem-solve. Open-ended toys allow children to be imaginative and explore aspects of reality. Montessori puzzles emphasize beauty, durability, and quality. There is guidance on learning about plants and animals from beautiful artworks, from observations in nature, and from animal models. Earth and physical sciences for children three to six-plus years looks at these subjects through hands-on experiences initially and then goes beyond to maps, globes, and pictures. To study the solar system, children are introduced through mobiles, puzzles, and later books. To study landforms, children create them in sand. Exploring physics and chemistry can be based on simple science experiments using candles, magnets, and water. Then this initial understanding is built upon.

Rudolf Steiner Schools

The Waldorf school movement grew out of the First World War as a basis for democratic equality and spiritual freedom of the individual. Rudolf Steiner, a philosopher, humanitarian, and scientist, first opened a school for blue- and white-collar workers in 1919. The central philosophy of these schools is to inculcate individuals as world citizens and as ethical human beings. An essay by Rudolf Steiner is available at http://www.peace.ca/waldorfschools.htm, as well as a response to critics in California who came from rationalist, secular humanist perspectives and Christian fundamentalist right-wing perspectives. There are other general links on Waldorf education with online articles. Another Web site, http://www.steiner-australia.org, provides recommended readings and a detailed overview of Steiner education.

Steiner schools balance the curriculum in terms of the academic, artistic, and social aspects of learning and different subject areas. Each child is regarded as an individual and children are encouraged to act as children, that is, according to the Steiner conceptualization of what constitutes childlike behavior. Free, creative play is encouraged, as well as artistic endeavors. Practical life skills are also taught. The curriculum is based on child development phases and on encouraging children's imagination, creativity, and free thinking. It is opposed to schooling based on functionalist demands of governments or industry. Encouraging children to develop their intellectual, emotional, and moral selves and to take initiative in their own lives is central to the philosophy.

There are three golden rules for teachers: "to receive the child in gratitude from the world they come from; to educate the child with love; and to lead the child into the true freedom that belongs to man." Steiner schools are distinctive in that teachers stay with children for six years after they enter school.

Artistic expression is used to promote flexible thinking, imagination, and lateral thinking for problem solving. Verbal communication is developed through storytelling, listening, illustrating, and acting. Writing is first developed through learning letters in terms of meanings, such as *M* for *mountain* or *V* for *valley*. Students walk the shape on the floor and draw pictures including the shape, write words, and read their writing. Learning numbers is based on practical tasks such as cutting up a cake, musical rhythms, and games. Literature is chosen from different mythologies and folk tales to enhance students' understanding of history and civilizations. The main lesson covers the major subjects taught for two hours per day. The spiritual aspect of Steiner education is about the sacred beauty and wonder of life. Eurythmy is a dancelike art form that involves expression of sound through movement for development of coordination and enhancing social connections between students. Steiner schools do not generally introduce computers or any electronic media until secondary school, though they are introduced near the end of primary school for children entering mainstream secondary schools. They argue that they are not appropriate or relevant for young children. On another Web site on Waldorf schools there are references to research criticizing computers and mass media in childhood (http://hem.passagen.se/thebee/waldorf/links2.htm?k), as well as general references on Steiner education.

CONCLUSION

There are many exemplars of effective integration of ICT in classrooms and early childhood centers, and increasingly there is an emphasis on the need to rethink basic foundational skills, pedagogies, and curricula. There are even moves to reassess how to fundamentally change the school environment to alter the social dynamics within classrooms and schools to enhance creativity, collaboration, and self-directed learning around projects. This book shows how some policy makers are starting to recognize how outdated our education systems have become in adapting to rapid social, economic, and technological change. Unfortunately, there has also been a countertrend in policy circles, with governments continuously promoting a back-to-basics approach that emphasizes rote learning rather than learning how to learn, and extending individual capacities to higher-order thinking and being able to apply knowledge. Additionally, groups such as the Alliance for Childhood and the Steiner schools oppose the integration of new technologies into early childhood and primary education. The resources in this chapter reinforce the argument throughout this book that there is a need to seriously reassess curricula, pedagogies, and school environments in ways that match the requirements of the information age. New technologies are tools that enhance and add to existing ways to explore ideas, create, research, and disseminate new knowledge acquired in the classroom. They provide opportunities to engage students and to draw on their diverse learning styles. This book draws together research that convincingly shows that we can create learning environments for children that are engaging, challenging, and fun. Meaningful learning becomes the basis for lifelong and lifewide learning that enables children to become adults who can cope with rapid social, technological, and economic change. It is clear that there is a need for a quite radical transformation of our education systems, and this book provides a glimmer of hope through exemplars and policy initiatives that are innovative and forward-looking.

Appendix 1
THE TECHNO TOUR

HOME VISITS: ISSUES AND QUESTIONS

- What do children include in their techno tour? Is it all technology ICT, or are all "machines" ICT? Where do we draw the line? Is a phone ICT? The definition of ICT includes the presence of a digital (central) processing unit that takes information in, processes it in some way, stores it, and then outputs it in some form.
- Does the child focus on any particular technologies?
- Where are the various technologies located?
- If a video recorder is included in the techno tour, what levels of competence or use are displayed? Is a remote used? Can the child set the video recorder to record a program at the correct time?
- If a computer is available to the child, what does the child like to do with it? Who decides? If you are watching a child playing a game or doing something else on the computer, can the child explain to you what he or she is doing?
- How is the child making the connections between conceptualizations of technologies and what he or she is showing you as you go around the home with the child?
- What prominence is given to the various ICTs in the home?
- What activities does the child like doing at home? Does the child incorporate the use of ICT, or is the child more traditional, engaging in activities such as painting or drawing, or playing with dolls or trucks?

- Who owns the technology?
- Do siblings, parents, grandparents, or other household members influence the use of ICT in the home?
- Are there any gender or class issues around the use of technology in the child's home?
- What assumptions are there around the use of technologies? Is the child given opportunities to engage with the technologies in ways that he or she chooses, or are the experiences shaped by those who designed the software and/or hardware?

Appendix 2
MATHEMATICAL TASKS CONTINUUM

1. USING MATHEMATICAL CONCEPTS AND PROCESSES

STRUCTURED USE	*OPEN-ENDED USE*
• The task requires a single outcome and usually only one way is accepted to achieve it. • The teacher has structured the task for the learner to use and practice a particular process or concept. • The children complete the task requirement(s) and do not deviate from set goal(s). • Children are not challenged to go beyond the single outcome or level achieved. • Traditional media are used (pencil, paper).	• The task allows for problem-solving and problem-posing opportunities in open-ended investigations. • The children share strategies and have input into the direction of their learning. • Children are motivated and inspired to investigate and try out ideas. • The children have opportunities to experience challenges. • The children and teacher integrate various media, including ICT.

→

2. APPLYING MATHEMATICAL KNOWLEDGE

FOCUSED APPLICATION	*EXTENDED APPLICATION*
• Specific mathematical concepts and processes are introduced via structured tasks. • The application or use is not integrated with other knowledge. • Few connections are made between the task and the children's prior understandings.	• The children apply a range of mathematical concepts and processes. • Application of knowledge is integrated. • Connections are made and encouraged between the task and the children's prior understandings. • The children use their own initiative and draw on a broad range of knowledge and processes to complete the task.

3. OPPORTUNITIES FOR EXPLORATION

MINIMAL OPPORTUNITIES	*MULTIPLE OPPORTUNITIES*
• Children are mostly taught in large groups (whole-class instruction). • The task is mostly teacher-directed and completed individually. • The children are encouraged not to deviate from a predetermined instructional plan. • Children respond with yes/no answers or closed/fixed answers. • Child mainly learn the process or concept in isolation. • The children may not show interest in the task if the concept is already known and the solution is a mechanical application of the skill.	• Children have ample time in large and small groups and on their own to conceptualize, plan, and reflect. • The children engage and lead discussion about their learning. • Tasks are initiated and/or extended by the child. • The structure of the session is flexible. • Children can approach the task in different ways. • The children can learn additional and complementary processes and mathematical concepts during task solution. • Collaborative and cooperative learning is encouraged. • The children find the task meaningful and are interested.

→

4. LEARNING OUTCOMES

LIMITED LEARNING OUTCOME(S)	VARIED LEARNING OUTCOMES
• The children's work looks the same. • The learning processes are specific to the task. • There are right and wrong answers and particular processes to follow. • Opportunity to use initiative is limited. • The children's own interpretations and learning extensions are not recognized as valid. • Communication of findings is not valued as a learning outcome.	• The children choose different media to represent and communicate their ideas and knowledge. • The children's learning processes are varied. • There are multiple solutions and outcome levels. • The children develop confidence in their own learning initiatives. • The children's additional learning is recognized as valid and important. • The children communicate their findings to others.

REFERENCES

ACER (Australian Council for Educational Research) (1990). *Being numerate: What counts?* Victoria, Australia: ACDE.

A. C. Nielsen (2005). Can you buy intelligence for your children? 50 percent of Hong Kong parents believe they can. A. C. Nielsen Asia Pacific news release, Hong Kong, April 26.

Amabile, T. (1988). A model of creativity and innovation in organizations. In *Research in organizational behavior,* ed. B. M. Staw and L. L. Cunnings. Greenwich, CT: JAI.

Anning, A., and A. Edwards (1999). *Promoting young children's learning from birth to five.* Buckingham: Open University Press.

Apple, M. (2001). *Educating the right way.* New York: Routledge.

Australian Council of Deans of Education (2001). *New learning: A charter for Australian Education.* Melbourne: ACDE.

Bangemann, M. (1994). *Europe and the global information society: Recommendations to the European Council.* Available at http://europa.eu.int/ISPO/infosoc/backg/bangeman.html#chap1.

Baroody, A., and J. L. M. Wilkins (1999). The development of informal counting, number, and arithmetic skills and concepts. In *Mathematics in the early years,* ed. J. V. Copley. Reston, VA: NCTM.

Battista, M. T., and D. H. Clements (1986). The effects of Logo and CAI problem-solving environments on problem-solving abilities and mathematics achievement. *Computers in Human Behavior* 2: 183–93.

Becta (2002). *ImpaCT2: Pupils' and teachers' perceptions of ICT in the home, school and community.* London: British Educational Communications and Technology Agency.

Beeman, C. A. (1990). *Just this side of madness: Creativity and the drive to create.* Conway, AR: University of Central Arkansas Press.

Blanton, W. E., G. B. Moorman, B. A. Hayes, and M. L. Warner (2000). Effects of participation in the Fifth Dimension on far transfer. *Journal of Educational Computing Research* 16: 371–96.

Brown, J. S., A. Collins, and P. Duguid (1989). Situated cognition and the culture of learning. *Educational Researcher* 18, 1: 32–42.

Bruner, J. (1977). *The process of education.* Cambridge, MA: Harvard University Press.

Buckingham, D., and M. Scanlon (2003). *Education, entertainment and learning in the home.* Buckingham: Open University Press.

Cassell, J., and H. Jenkins (1998). *From Barbie to Mortal Kombat: Gender and computer games.* Cambridge, MA: MIT Press.

Castells, M. (1996). *The rise of the network society.* Oxford: Blackwell.

Cazden, C. (2001). *Classroom discourse: The language of teaching and learning.* Portsmouth, NH: Heinemann.

Chandler-Olcott, K. and Mahar, P. (2003). Tech-saviness meets multiliteracies: exploring adult girls' technology-mediated practices. *Reading Research Quarterly* 38, 356–385.

Clay, M. M. (1993). *An observation survey: of early literacy achievement.* Auckland: Heinemann.

Clements, D. H. (1987). Longitudinal study of the effects of Logo programming on cognitive abilities and achievement. *Journal of Educational Computing Research* 3, 1: 73–94.

——— (1999). Concrete manipulatives, concrete ideas. *Contemporary Issues in Early Childhood* 1, 1: 45–60.

Clements, D. H., et al. (1995). *Turtle paths.* Palo Alto, CA: Dale Seymour.

——— (1997). Students' development of length concepts in a Logo-based unit on geometric paths. *Journal for Research in Mathematics* 28, 1: 70–95.

Clements, D. H., and M. T. Battista (1994). Computer environments for learning geometry. *Journal of Educational Research* 10, 2: 173–97.

Clements, D. H., and S. McMillen (1996). Rethinking concrete manipulatives. *Teaching Children Mathematics*, January, 270–353.

Clements, D. H., B. K. Nastasi, and S. Swaminathan (1993). Young children and computers: Crossroads and directions from research. *Young Children* 48, 2: 56–64.

Cole, M. (1996). *Cultural Psychology.* Cambridge, MA: Harvard University Press.

Cope, B., and M. Kalantzis (2000). *Multiliteracies: Literacy, learning and the design of social futures.* Melbourne: Macmillan.

Craft, A., B. Jeffrey, and M. Leibling, eds. (2001). *Creativity in education.* London: Continuum.

Cross, G. (2004). *Kids' stuff: Toys and the changing world of American childhood.* Cambridge, MA: Harvard University Press.

Csikszentmihalyi, M. (1996). *Creativity: Flow and the psychology of discovery and invention.* New York: Harper Perennial.

Cuban, L. (1993). Computers meet classroom: Classroom wins. *Teachers College Record* 95, 2: 185–219.

——— (2001). *Oversold and underused: Computers in the classroom.* Cambridge, MA: Harvard University Press.

Dapin, M. (2006). Have we done our homework? *The Good Weekend (Sydney Morning Herald)*, February 25, 32–38.

Darling-Hammond, L. (2001). *A right to learn: A blueprint for creating schools that work.* San Francisco: Jossey Bass.

Dede, C. (2000). Commentary: Looking at the future. *The Future of Children* 10, 2: 178–80.

De Jean, J., R. Upitis, C. Koch, and J. Young (1999). The story of the phoenix quest: How girls respond to a prototype language and mathematics computer game. *Gender and Education* 11, 2: 207–223.

Department for Culture, Media, and Sport (2001). *Culture and creativity: The next ten years.* London: Department for Culture, Media, and Sport.

Department of Education and Children's Services (2001). SACSA Curriculum Framework. Government of South Australia, Department of Education and Children's Services.

Department of Education, Queensland (2001). *New basics: The why. what, how and when of rich tasks.* Brisbane: Access Education.

Department of Education and Employment (DFEE). (1997). *Connecting the Learning Society.* London: DFEE.

Department of Education, Training, and Youth Affairs (2000). Numeracy, a priority for all: Challenges for Australian schools. Canberra: ACT, DETYA.

Devlin, K. (2000). The four faces of mathematics. In *Learning mathematics for a new century,* ed. M. J. Burke and F. R. Curcio. Reston, VA: NCTM.

DFC Intelligence (2005). Interactive entertainment industry to rival size of global music business. DFC Intelligence press release, November 9.

Diezmann, C., and J. Watters (2000). Identifying and supporting spatial intelligence in young children. *Contemporary Issues in Early Childhood* 1, 3: 299–313.

Donnelly, K. (2006). Let's go back to basics, beginning with the three R's. *The Australian,* January 31.

Downes, T., and C. Reddacliff (1996). Young children talking about computers in their homes. Paper presented at the 14th Australian Computers in Education Conference, Canberra.

Durrant, C., and Green, B. (2000). Literacy and the new technologies in school education: Meeting the l(IT)eracy challenge? *The Australian Journal of Language and Literacy* 23, 2: 89–108.

Eco, U. (1990). *Limits of interpretation.* Bloomington: Indiana University Press.

Edwards, L. (2002). Learning by design: Environments that support girls' learning with technology. In *Ghosts in the machine: Women's voices in research with technology,* ed. N. Yelland and A. Rubin. New York: Peter Lang.

Fleer, M. (2000). Visual thinking in technology education. In *Thinking through the arts,* ed. W. Schiller. Amsterdam: Harwood Academic Publishers.

Florida, R. (2003). *The rise of the creative class.* Melbourne: Pluto Press.

Forestier, K., and M. Chan (2004). Prowess in maths fails to add up to a happy sum total. *South China Morning Post,* December 8, A3.

Freire, P. (1972). *Pedagogy of the oppressed.* New York: Herder and Herder.

Gallas, K. (1995). *Talking their way into science: Hearing children's questions and theories, responding with curricula.* New York: Teachers College Press.

——— (2003). *Imagination and literacy: A teacher's search for the heart of learning.* New York: Teachers College Press.

Gardner, H. (2000). *Intelligence reframed: Multiple intelligences for the 21st century.* New York: Basic Books.

Gee, J. P. (2003). *What video games have to teach us about learning and literacy.* New York: Palgrave Macmillan.

——— (2004). *Situated language and learning: A critique of traditional schooling.* New York: Routledge.

Green, B., J. Reid, and C. Bigum (1999). Teaching the Nintendo generation? Children, computer culture and popular technologies. In *Wired up: Young people and the electronic media,* ed. S. Howard. London: Taylor and Francis.

Greenes, C. (1999). Ready to learn: Developing young children's mathematical powers. In J. V. Copley, ed., *Mathematics in the early years.* Reston, VA: NCTM.

Hall, S., and M. Jacques (1989). *New times: The changing face of politics in the 1990s.* London: Lawrence Wishart.

Handal, B., and A. Herrington (2003). Mathematics teachers' beliefs and curriculum reform. *Mathematics Education Research Journal* 15, 1: 59–69.

Harvey, D. (1989). *The condition of postmodernity: An inquiry into the origins of cultural change.* Oxford: Basil Blackwell.

Hayes, D., M. Mills, P. Christie, and B. Lingard (2006). *Teachers and schooling making a difference: Productive pedagogies, assessment and performance.* Crows Nest, New South Wales: Allen and Unwin.

Her Majesty's Inspectorate (1998). The national numeracy project: An HMI evaluation. London: Office of Her Majesty's Chief Inspector of Schools.

Hill, S., et al. (1998). *100 children go to school: Connections and disconnections in literacy development in the year prior to school and the first year of school.* Canberra: Department for Education, Employment, Training and Youth Affairs.

Hitchens, C. (2001). *Letters to a young contrarian.* Cambridge, MA: Basic Books.

Howe, N., and W. Strauss (2000). *Millennials rising: The next great generation.* New York: Vintage.

Hunting, R. P. (1999). Rational-number learning in the early years: What is possible? In *Mathematics in the early years,* ed. J. V. Copley. Reston, VA: NCTM.

Illich, I. (1971). *Deschooling society.* New York: Harper and Row.

Inkpen, K., et al. (1994). "We have never-forgetful flowers in our garden": Girls' responses to electronic games. *Journal of Computers in Mathematics and Science Teaching* 13, 4: 383–403.

Johnson, L. B. (1964). Remarks at the University of Michigan. Presidential address, May 22. Available at http://www.lbjlib.utexas.edu/johnson/archives.hom/speeches.hom/640522.asp.

Kaiser Family Foundation (1999). Kids and media @ the new millennium. Kaiser Family Foundation, Menlo Park, CA, www.kff.org/entmedia/1835-index.cfm.

———(2005). Generation M: Media in the lives of 8–18-year-olds. Kaiser Family Foundation, Menlo Park, CA, www.kff.org/entmedia/7251.cfm.

Kalantzis, M., and B. Cope (2005). *Learning by design.* Altona, Victoria: Standard Books/ Common Ground Publishing.

Katz, J. (1997). The rights of kids in the digital age. *Wired,* July.

Kling, R., and W. Scacchi (1982). The web of computing: Computer technology as social organization. *Advances in Computers* 21: 1–90.

Labbo, L. (1996). A semiotic analysis of young children's symbol making in a classroom computer centre. *Reading Research Quarterly* 31: 356–385.

Lankshear, C., and M. Knobel (2003). *New literacies: Changing knowledge and classroom learning.* Buckingham: Open University Press.

Learning Federation (2005). Learning objects catalogue. Learning Federation, Melbourne. Available at www.thelearningfederation.edu.au/tlf2/showMe.asp?nodeID=75.

Leitze, A. R. (1997). Connecting process problem solving to children's literature. *Teaching Children Mathematics* 3: 74–77.

Lemke, J. (1990). *Talking science: Language, learning, and values.* Norwood, NJ: Ablex Publishing Corporation.

Loveless, A. (2003). Creating spaces in the primary curriculum: ICT in creative subjects. *The Curriculum Journal* 14, 1: 5–21.

Luckin, R., D. Connolly, L. Plowman, and S. Airey (2003). With a little help from my friends: Children's interactions with interactive toy technology. *Journal of Computer Assisted Learning* 19, 2: 165–76.

Lyotard, J. F. (1984). *The postmodern condition: A report on knowledge.* Manchester: Manchester University Press.

McCreedy, C. N. J. (2004). The "creativity problem" and the future of the Japanese workforce. *Asia Program Special Report* (Woodrow Wilson International Center for Scholars, Washington, DC), June 1–3.

Meadows, S., and A. Cashdan (1988). *Helping children learn: Contributions to a cognitive curriculum.* London: David Fulton.

Ministerial Council on Education, Employment, Training, and Youth Affairs (1999). The Adelaide declaration on national goals for schooling in the twenty-first century. Department of Education, Training, and Youth Affairs, Australian Government. Available at http://www.dest.gov.au/sectors/school_education/policy_initiatives_reviews/national_goals_for_schooling_in_the_twenty_first_century.htm.

Moll, L. C., C. Amanti, D. Neff, and N. Gonzalez (1992). Funds of knowledge for teaching: Using a qualitative approach to connect homes and classrooms. *Theory into Practice* 31, 2: 132–41.

National Advisory Committee on Creative and Cultural Education (1999). All our futures: Creativity, culture and education. Department for Education and Skills, London. Available at http://www.dfes.gov.uk/naccce/index1.shtml.

NCTM (National Council of Teachers of Mathematics) (1989). Curriculum and evaluation standards for school mathematics. Reston, VA: NCTM.

———— (1995). *Assessment standards for school mathematics.* Reston, VA: NCTM.

———— (1998). Principles and standards for school mathematics: Discussion draft. NCTM, Reston, VA.

———— (2000). *Principles and standards for school mathematics: An Overview.* Reston, VA: NCTM.

Negroponte, N. (1995). *Being digital.* Rydalmere, NSW: Hodder and Stroughton.

New London Group (1996). A pedagogy of multiliteracies. *Harvard Educational Review* 60, 1: 66–92.

Nicolopoulou, A., and M. Cole (1993). Generation and transmission of shared knowledge in the culture of collaborative learning: The Fifth Dimension, its play world, and its institutional contexts. In *Contexts for learning: Sociocultural dynamics in children's development,* ed. E. A. Foreman, N. Minick, and C. A. Stone. New York: Oxford University Press.

OECD (2001). *Learning to change: ICT in schools.* Paris: OECD.

Papert, S. (1980). *Mindstorms: Children, computers, and powerful ideas.* Brighton, Sussex: Harvester.

———— (1996). *The connected family: Bridging the digital generation gap.* Atlanta: Longstreet Press.

Pellegrini, A. D. (1991). *Applied child study: A developmental approach.* Hillsdale, NJ: Lawrence Erlbaum.

Piaget, J. (1972). *The principles of genetic epistemology.* New York: Basic Books.

Piannfetti, E. (2001). Teachers and technology: Digital literacy through professional development. *Language Arts* 78, 3: 255–62.

Plowman, L., and C. Stephen (2005). Children, play, and computers in pre-school education. *British Journal of Educational Technology* 36, 2: 145–57.

Podmore, V., and M. Carr (1999). Learning and teaching stories: New approaches to assessment and evaluation. Paper presented at the AARE-NZARE Conference on Research in Education, Melbourne.

Postman, N. (1993). *Technopoly: The surrender of culture to technology.* New York: Vintage Books.

Pronsky, M. (2001). *Digital game-based learning.* New York, McGraw-Hill.

Provenzo, E. F. (1992). The video game generation. *American School Board Journal* 179, 3: 29–32.

Resnick, M. (2001). Revolutionizing learning in the digital age. EDUCAUSE: Forum for the Future of Higher Education, Boulder, CO, and Washington, DC.

Robinson, K. (2001). *Out of our minds: Learning to be creative.* Oxford: Capstone.

Robinson, K. (2005). *Backing our creativity keynote presentation.* National Education and the Arts Symposium, Melbourne, September 2005.

Roschelle, J., et al. (2000). Changing how and what children learn in school with computer-based technologies. *The Future of Children* 10, 2: 76–101.

RocSearch (2005). Video game industry. RocSearch, New York, March 1.

Scardamalia, M. (2003). Extending the limits of the possible in education. Keynote presentation, International Conference for Educational Technology, Hong Kong.

———— (2005). What are the conditions for learning that need to be in place for children to reach their full potential? Presentation at the Canadian Education Association symposium "What Do We Know About Early Learning and What Are We Doing About It," May 18, Toronto.

———— (nd). *Reflections on the transformation of education for the knowledge age.* Available at http://www3.usal.es/-teoneducation/vev_numero_05/n5_art_scardamalia.htm.

Scardamalia, M., and C. Bereiter (2003). Knowledge building. *Encyclopedia of Education.* New York: Macmillan Reference.

Schank, R. C. (2002). *Designing world-class e-learning.* New York: McGraw-Hill.

Shenk, D. (1997). *Data smog: Surviving the information glut.* New York: Harper Collins.

Steen, L. A. (1999). Numeracy: The new literacy for a data drenched society. *Educational Leadership* 57, 2: 8–13.

Straker, A. (2000). The National Numeracy Project. In the issues in teaching numeracy in primary schools. I. Thompson (Ed.). pp. 39-48. Buckingham, UK: OUP.

Strommen, E., and K. Alexander (1999). *Learning from television with interactive toy characters as viewing companions.* Paper presented at the annual meeting of the Society for Research in Child Development, Albuquerque, New Mexico.

Sylva, K., C. Roy, and M. Painter (1980). *Childwatching at playgroup and nursery school.* London: McIntyre.

Tinker, R. (1999). New technology bumps into an old curriculum: Does the traditional course sequence need an overhaul? *@Concord,* newsletter of the Concord Consortium, Concord, MA, winter.

Toy Industry Association (2004). 2004 vc. 2003 state of the industry. Available at http://www.toy-tia.org/content/navigationmenu/press_room/statistics3/state_of_the_Industry/2004_vs_2003.htm.

Upitis, R. (1998). From hackers to Luddites, game players to game creators: Profiles of adolescent students using technology. *Journal of Curriculum Studies* 30, 3: 293–318.

U.S. Department of Education (2001). No child left behind. Jessup, MD: Educational Publications Center.

——— (2005). U.S. Department of Education Releases National Education Technology Plan. Press release, January 7. Available at http://www.ed.gov/news/pressreleases/2005/01/01072005.html.

Victorian Curriculum and Assessment Authority (2005). The Victorian Essential Learning Standards. Victorian Curriculum and Assessment Authority, East Melbourne.

Vygotsky, L. S. (1978). *Mind in society: The development of higher psychological processes.* Cambridge, MA: Harvard University Press.

Warschauer, M. (2002). Reconceptualizing the digital divide. *First Monday* 7, 7.

——— (2004). *Technology and social inclusion: Rethinking the digital divide.* Cambridge, MA: MIT Press.

Willis, S. (1998). *Which numeracy?* Unicorn, Vol. 24(2), 32-41.

Yelland, N. J. (1993). National testing at 7: What can we learn from the UK experience. Paper presented at the annual meeting of the Australian Early Childhood Association, Brisbane.

——— (1997). Young children's understanding of paths and measurement. *Mathematics Education Research Journal* 10, 1: 83–99.

——— (1998). Empowerment and control with technology for young children. *Educational Theory and Practice* 20, 2: 45–55.

——— (1999). Reconceptualising schooling with technology for the 21st Century: Images and reflections. *Information Technology in Childhood Education Annual* (AACE, Charlottesville, VA), 39–59.

——— (2002a). Creating microworlds for exploring mathematical understandings in the early years of school. *Journal of Educational Computing Research* 27, 1–2: 77–92.

——— (2002b). Playing with ideas and games in early mathematics. *Contemporary Issues in Early Childhood Education* 3, 2: 197–215.

——— (2002c). Asdf; lkjh: Challenges to early childhood curriculum and pedagogy in the information age. In *ICT in the primary school,* ed. A. Loveless and B. Dore. Buckingham: Open University Press.

———— (2003). Making connections with powerful ideas in measurement and length. In *Learning and Teaching Measurement. 2003 Yearbook.* Ed. DH Clements and G. Bright (pp. 31–45). Reston, VA: NCTM.

———— (2005). Curriculum, pedagogies and practice with ICT in the information age. In *Critical issues in early childhood education,* ed. N. J. Yelland. Buckingham: Open University Press.

Yi, M. (2004). They got game: Stacks of new releases for hungry video game enthusiasts mean it's boom time for an industry now even bigger than Hollywood. *San Francisco Chronicle,* December 18.

Zevenbergen, R. (2004). Technologizing numeracy: Intergenerational differences in working mathematically in new times. *Education Studies in Mathematics* 56: 97–117.

INDEX

M

Machines, as objects to think with, 9
Manual workers, disenfranchisement of, 7
Mass media images, multiliteracies in, 37
Massachusetts Institute of Technology Media Lab, 149, 161–162
Mastery, in video games, 84
Math Workshop, 77
Mathematical literacy, 89
  applying mathematical knowledge, 178
  Building Blocks and, 159
  Clements on, 159–160
  exploration opportunities, 178
  learning outcomes, 179
  and mental computational skills, 90
  using mathematical concepts/ processes, 177
Mathematics
  computer games as stimulus for engagement with, 80
  establishing positive attitudes towards, 88
  five content areas, 32–33
  incorporating computer games into, 92
  learning through step sizes, 61
  and length/angle measurements, 61
  as method of reasoning, 25
  multidimensional tasks in, 102
  new standards for, 32–37
  play involving, 61–62
  teachers' concept of, 95–100, 98, 100
  understanding through computer games, 77
  use of computer games in, 74
Mathematics skills, 5
Meaning making, 2, 8, 112, 148
  DATEC Project, 148–149
  in pedagogy of multiliteracies, 38
  in presence of adult guidance, 51
  and Screenplay project, 156
  technology as play in, 49
Measurable outcomes, 9
Measurement
  as emphasis in National Numeracy Project, 88
  with new technologies, 61–62
  relative importance in numeracy skills, 90

Media
  children's average use of, 3
  millenials' use of, 3–4
Media literacy, 149
  and U.K. regulatory policy, 150
Media regulation, 150
Media saturation, 136, 150
Memorization, international test focus on, 121
Mental computation, as foundational skill, 90
Messenger software, 2
Michelin view of assessment, 45
Microsoft Office software, 2
Microworlds, use in mathematics education, 33–35
Migrant workers, disenfranchisement of, 7
Millenials, 1–3, 111–119, 136
  Alliance for Childhood, 142–143
  British Educational Communications and Technology Agency (BECTA), 141
  Kaiser Family Foundation and, 136–137
  National Grid for Learning initiative, 141–142
  and new technologies and media, 3–4
  OECD, 138
  UNESCO, 137–138
  U.S. Department of Education policy, 139–141
Minibeast project, 109–111
Montessori education, 49, 170–171
  structured play in, 50
Moviemaker, 2
Multidimensional tasks, 102
Multiliteracies, 29, 37, 40, 44, 124, 146, 157
  pedagogy of, 38, 112
  role in new basics curriculum, 28
Multimedia presentations, as rich task assessment, 29
Multimodality, 158–159
Multiple-choice questions, 7
Multisensory learning
  in Montessori schools, 170
  in Reggio Emilia schools, 167
My Make Believe Castle software, 54
My Very First Farm, 55